LOVE ME...PLEASE

First Book in the LOVE ME, TOUCH ME, HEAL ME **Series**

The Path to Physical, Emotional

Sexual and Spiritual Reawakening

Dr. Erica Goodstone

Copyright © 2009, Revised 2023   *Love Me ... Please*   DrEricaGoodstone.com

Love Me ... Please, **Book One in the series, is dedicated to**

- **Hilda Aronson, for helping me to get started**
- **Bryce Britton-Kranz, my colleague, mentor and friend, who provided support and lasting friendship that has sustained me over the years**
- **Glenn Dietzel's Awakened team, for pushing me to completion**

Publisher Data & Legal Information

Copyright © 2009 by Erica Goodstone, Ph.D. All rights reserved.
ISBN: 978-0-9824304-4-6
Published by Create Healing and Love Now Publishers
Contact the Publisher at RelationshipHealingToolboxcom

All rights reserved. No part of this eBook may be reproduced, stored in a retrieval system or transmitted in any form or by any means electronic, mechanical, photocopying, recording, or otherwise without express written permission of the author.

Every attempt has been made by the author to provide acknowledgement of the sources used for the material in this book. If there has been an omission of any source, please contact the author at
DrErica@DrEricaWellness.com

Disclaimer: No responsibility is assumed by the authors/publishers for any injury and/or damage and/or loss sustained in persons or property as a result of using this product; and/or for any liability, negligence or otherwise use or operation of any products, methods, instructions or ideas contained in the material herein.

The views and opinions expressed in this book and related materials are derived from the author's experience and research as a professor of health and physical education, yoga and meditation teacher, licensed mental health counselor, licensed professional counselor, licensed marriage and family therapist, board certified sex therapist, licensed massage and bodywork therapist, certified pain management practitioner, certified Integrative Medicine practitioner, certified Polarity Therapist, certified Rubenfeld Synergist, and involvement with numerous professional associations. She is not a licensed M.D. and does not diagnose or claim to cure any physical disease. She is also not a psychiatrist and does not claim to cure mental illness.

Any reader currently under the care or supervision of a psychiatrist, physician or other medical or behavioral health practitioner is urged to seek their professional advice before using or practicing any of the material or techniques contained herein.

Copyright © 2009, Revised 2023   *Love Me … Please*   DrEricaGoodstone.com

ABOUT THE AUTHOR

Erica Goodstone, Ph.D., has devoted her life's work to the discovery of love, healing and the creation of intimate, satisfying, fulfilling and joyful relationships. During over two decades, through her lectures, seminars and private counseling sessions, she has worked with thousands of men and women to create love and healing in their lives.

Having studied extensively from many different sources, Dr. Goodstone is a licensed mental health counselor, professional counselor, marriage and family therapist, massage and bodywork therapist. She is a diplomate and fellow for the American Association of Integrative Medicine and a diplomate for the American Academy of Pain Management. Dr. Goodstone is also a diplomate for the American Board of Sexology, a fellow for the American Academy of Clinical Sexologists, and a certified Sex Therapist for the American Association of Sexuality Educators and Therapists.

As a former professor of health and physical education at F.I.T./State University of New York, Dr. Goodstone spent 25 years studying and teaching about the body: physical fitness, health and wellness, stress management, sports psychology, team building and human sexuality. But she did not stop there.

Dr. Goodstone also spent many years studying a wide variety of healing body therapy modalities in including massage, shiatsu, polarity therapy, craniosacral therapy, Reiki, reflexology, Chinese medical theory, Japanese healing theories. Her studies led to the combination of touch with counseling through the gentle yet profound Rubenfeld Synergy Method. In fact, she was on the original steering committee and the board of directors

Copyright © 2009, Revised 2023 *Love Me … Please* DrEricaGoodstone.com

for the first two terms of the U.S. Association for Body Psychotherapy. This was the first organization to bring together
all the different originators and practitioners of somatic body psychotherapy methods and modalities.

But Dr. Goodstone's knowledge and background does not stop there. She has also fervently and passionately craved her own inner spiritual development and outer social awareness. Her seeking led her to spend many years studying yoga, first with the Sivananda Center in New York City and at the Sivananda Ashram in Paradise Island, Bahamas, where she met Swami Vishnu Devananda and listened to Ravi Shankar play the sitar. Later she spent years working with Guru Mayi, Swami Muktananda's disciple, receiving Darshan and personl counseling as needed.

Her studies included attending many consciousness raising seminars in the 1980's, including the EST seminars led by Werner Erhard, the Living Love Workshops led by Ken Keyes, Jr., author of *The Handbook to Higher Consciousness,* and DMA seminars about the creative process and structural thinking led by Robert Fritz. She avidly studied the Rosicrucian manuals for many years, along with the Kaballah teachings of *The Builders of the Adytum* and *The Course in Miracles*. Her current focus has been upon the works of Joel Goldsmith, *The Infinite Way,* and Swami Muktananda, Siddha Yogi Guru..

Dr. Erica Goodstone has been a celebrated speaker at national and local professional and public events. Since her doctoral dissertation, which studied the effects of early mother-infant bonding upon later adult intimacy, she has continued to write extensively about creating love through the healing power of touch, intimacy, and the mind/body/spirit connection.

Dr. Goodstone's interviews and articles have appeared in *Who's Who of Medicine and Healthcare, CBS 4 TV, Blog Talk Radio Logical Soul Talk, Mademoiselle, Cosmopolitan , Marie Claire, Penthouse Forum, Journal of Sex and Marital therapy, Newsletters of the U.S. Association for Body Psychotherapy.* Dr. Goodstone has a very wide presence on the web. Her bio and blogs appear on numerous sites, e.g., Wordpress.com and Gather.com, as well as numerous ezines, most notably ezinearticles.com

Dr. Goodstone's chapter, "Sexual Reawakening" appears in the wonderfully organized book of Rubenfeld Synergy practitioners, *Healing Journeys: The Power of Rubenfeld Synergy, V. Mechner, Ed.* She has also written a section about touch therapies in the internationally acclaimed book, *The Continuum Complete International Encyclopedia of Sexuality*, R. J Noonan and R. Francoeur, Eds.

IN 2012, Dr. Erica published her first novel, **Love in the Blizzard of Life**, a sexy romantic novel about two star crossed lovers proving that where there is love there IS a way.

Dr. Goodstone can be reached at

DrErica@DrEricaWellness.com

****

Copyright © 2009, Revised 2023   *Love Me … Please*   DrEricaGoodstone.com

INTRODUCTION To The Series

Love Me, Touch Me, Heal Me: The Path to Physical, Emotional, Sexual and Spiritual Reawakening shows us what it takes to love, touch, and heal our own self. As we heal, we develop a renewed passion for life, a deep sense of being connected to something beyond our immediate life circumstances, and an increased desire for intimate loving. ***Love Me, Touch Me, Heal Me*** is meant to be a coming out party, coming out of hiding, bringing our total self into the light for examination, acceptance, and readiness to share our authentic self intimately with others.

Clients, colleagues and friends have often asked me to recommend a good book about love and relationships or about emotional intimacy and sexual communication. Others have requested information about ways to heal their body through natural methods, e.g., diet, exercise, body therapy, or even spirituality. And some have wondered what the best psychological approach might be to overcome fears, anxiety, anger, depression or relationship conflicts.

Answers to the above questions will be easily obtained as you read through this series of four books. You will discover that you can find the answers to most of your problems, dilemmas, life issues and concerns through self-evaluation. As you complete the exercises, you will literally begin to heal your cellular memories, create new brain patterns and remove lifelong blocks to intimate joyful relating. You can turn to professionals for expert opinions, guidance, support and mentoring, but with this book you will begin to more fully trust your own inner knowing about what is truly best for your growth and healing.

FORMAT OF THIS BOOK

This **Book Series** is divided into four books consisting of three chapters in each book as follows:

Book I	Love Me … Please	
	Chapter 1	The Gift of Love
	Chapter 2	Be Who You Are The Greatest Gift of All
	Chapter 3	The Delicate Dance of Love
Book II	Touch Me … Please	
	Chapter 1	Your Body Believes You
	Chapter 2	It's a Sensational World
	Chapter 3	Touching Matters The Profound Effects of Body Therapy
Book III	Heal Me … Please	
	Chapter 1	Heal Me…Please
	Chapter 2	Let All Your Senses Speak…As You Heal
	Chapter 3	Touching Stories Healing Through Body Psychotherapy
Book IV	Sexual and Spiritual Reawakening	
	Chapter 1	Ordinary People Ordinary Yet Extraordinary Sex
	Chapter 2	Ten Simple Steps to Sexual Reawakening
	Chapter 3	Sexual And Spiritual Reawakening At Last

Copyright © 2009, Revised 2023   *Love Me … Please*   DrEricaGoodstone.com

- Every chapter contains vital information, theories, concepts and suggestions gleaned from years of study, research, personal and professional experiences.

- Every chapter includes pertinent real-life stories, individual and partner written, verbal and contemplative exercises.

- Every chapter builds upon the previous one in the healing process.

- Every chapter is also complete unto itself.

- You may choose to read one entire book from start to finish and then begin a second book.

- You may choose to start with a specific chapter in any of the books.

- Resources, references, and keywords will appear at the end of each book.

Written many years ago, this book has been hibernating in file boxes until now, a time when this world needs all the love we can muster. This book teaches us how to let go of preconceived ideas as we learn the true art of loving.

Love Me, Touch Me, Heal Me: The Path to Physical, Emotional, Sexual and Spiritual Reawakening belongs in the personal library of anyone who truly wants to heal from the past and create loving, touching and authentically intimate relationships. This is a guidebook, a reference book, and a comforting friend along the path to reawakening.

HOW TO USE THIS BOOK

This book is about your life, my life, and all of our lives. Read this book, follow the exercises, and watch miracles happen. *Love Me, Touch Me, Heal Me* is a life transforming healing process. For best results, you will need a few basic materials.

1. **Writing Materials**

   a. **A journal, preferably a beautiful, special journal, but any 4" by 6" or 8" by 10" lined or unlined, notebook will do.** Choosing a journal or notebook that is special to you creates an experience of sensory stimulation every time you write in it! If you choose to write all the exercises in this book on pieces of paper, that's okay. But, if the outer appearance is appealing and soothing to your eyes, if the texture satisfies your sense of touch, if there's a fragrance of fresh cut paper or soft smooth leather that comforts you, the power of the words you write will be enhanced. Your brain will connect the sensual beauty of your journal with your written words and with your life. Your mind and body will begin to believe that you are serious about creating healing, love, spiritual connection, sexual aliveness, and joy in your life.

b. **Pen, pencil, colored pencils or crayons.**

Brain research indicates that the mind absorbs information best when all the senses are involved. So get yourself a box of colored pencils, colored pens or crayons. You'll probably discover that you want some pastels, and maybe even paint and brushes before you're through. Colors and textures add additional dimensionality to your writing, increasing the possibility for your brain to record and store your hopes and dreams, uplifting words, goals, new beliefs, and appropriate affirmations. This allows your mind, at a later point in time, to easily refute your fears, frustrations and anxieties as they arise in your consciousness. Crayons and colored pencils may also stimulate your brain to create images, faces, doodles, and other self-expressions that reveal some important subconscious personal thought

Processes.

2. **_A quiet place, even a corner of a room, set aside to practice the exercises._**

   Energy accumulates in a space that you set aside and use specifically for one purpose. Creating a special place for your own inner work is a strong suggestion to your subconscious, (the part of your brain that allows your dreams to germinate into fruition), that you are serious about transforming your life.

3. **_Recording Materials_**

   Choose your own recording device.

   To do the exercises in this book, you can read and stop, read and stop, or you can record your own voice first. Then you will be able to go straight through the exercise without stopping. The goal is for you to comfort yourself and love yourself. Hearing your own voice is a powerful affirmation that you can create what you want and you are all you will ever truly need.

As you begin your journey along the path to love, take a moment to assess where you are right now in your life. The questions you are about to answer may seem simple but are actually quite profound. Observe your thoughts. Notice any automatic body responses you may have. You are more than your thoughts. You are more than your body. Allow your automatic responses to help you to discover who you truly are.

For all the exercises in this introduction and in the rest of this book, you have choices. You can read the exercise and then write in your journal. You can record the entire exercise with your own voice, close the book, close your eyes, and visualize freely. Or, you can listen to the pre-recorded audio tapes that accompany each chapter.

Copyright © 2009, Revised 2023 *Love Me … Please* DrEricaGoodstone.com

Who Are You?

Sit in a comfortable position.

Inhale slowly, very slowly, and deeply.

Exhale slower than your usual rate.

Take three slow, deep, easy, and quiet breaths.

Close your eyes and allow your body to relax.

Take three more slow, deep, easy, and quiet breaths.

Open your eyes only to read each question.

Immediately close your eyes and allow the answer to come to you.

Accept the answers that come. Do not edit or change the response

Listen to your mind's first answer, the most correct response at this moment.

> *Who am I?*
>
> *What are other people here for in my life?*
>
> *Why am I alive now?*
>
> *What do I believe about love?*
>
> *Who do I enjoy touching and for what purpose?*
>
> *What yearns to heal inside of me?*
>
> *What does sexual reawakening mean to me?*
>
> *What is the role of God, a higher power, or spirituality in my life?*

Copyright © 2009, Revised 2023   *Love Me … Please*   DrEricaGoodstone.com

TABLE OF CONTENTS

PART ONE   *LOVE ME … PLEASE*

Introduction To The Series……………….....7
    Format of The Book
    How To Use This Book
    Who Are You?

Table of Contents……………………….....16

***Love Me … Please* Introduction**………....19
    Love Is All There Is ……………………..20
    Love Me Please Poem……………………24

Chapter 1   *THE GIFT OF LOVE*…………27
    Love Is All There Is ……………………..29
        Love And Intimacy Are Healing
        Betty's Husband Leaves
        Intimacy Is Not For The Faint Of Heart
        Separation-Individuation
        Good Enough Mothering And Fathering
        Emotions Signal Unmet Needs
        What Are Your Nurturing Needs?
        How Have You Loved?
        How Do You Love Others When You Feel Unloved?
        How Have You Loved Yourself?
    I Love/I Hate………………………………..46
        Beliefs
        I Believe
        Conflicting Beliefs
        Changing Beliefs
        How Do I Express My Emotions?

What is My Loving Potential?
Letter to My Birth Mother or Earliest Caretaker
The Mother of My Dreams
Letter to My Birth Father or Earliest Father Figure
The Father of My Dreams

What Are Your Rules For Loving?..........................59
This is MY Life?
What are My Rules for Loving?
The Eraser Game
My New Rules for Creative Loving

Chapter 2 BE WHO YOU ARE
THE GREATEST GIFT OF ALL...66

Who Are You?...72
Who Am I?
Who Are You?
Who Is (Your Name)?
Who Have You Been Told You Are?

How Have Others' Opinions Affected You?..............76
How have You Taken a Stand for Yourself?
Playing Roles
What Roles Have You Played?
How Did You Become Who You Are?
Your Family At Home
Your Family At The Dinner Table

Your Creative Expression……………………………..83
Drawing, Painting and Sculpting
Moving Your Body, Dancing and Being Athletic
Cooking, Sewing and Cleaning
Inventing, Building, Repairing, Doing Mathematical
    Or Electrical Work
Speaking, Singing, Playing an Instrument, Acting,
    Being a Comic, Being a Clown
Your Creative Expression Collage
Sculpting Yourself -Removing That Which Is Not You

Who Are You?...92

Chapter 3   THE DELICATE DANCE OF LOVE..94

My Romantic Fantasy……………………………………99
    Why Do I Want A Love Relationship?
    What Do I Believe About Love Relationships?
    What Do I Expect To Receive From A Love
        Relationship?
    What Do I Expect To Give To A Love Relationship?
Love Is The Essence Of Life……………………….108
    How Will I Love Today?
    Have I Given Up On Love?
    The Way Out
Don't Pass The Test Of Abuse…………………..…117
    Red Flags Of Abuse
    What Is Sexual Abuse?
    Don't Rescue Anyone
    Getting Free
    Forgiveness
Being Love……………………………………….…..127
    Love Changes Everything
    The Basic Decision To Love
    What Is Intimacy?
    Creating Intimacy
    Lover's Bill Of Rights
    It's The Little Things That Count
Footnotes …………………………………………..…137
More To Come………………………………………....138
Also by Dr. Erica Goodstone…………………….141

LOVE ME ... PLEASE

BOOK ONE

INTRODUCTION

Love me, please

I don't deserve it

Love me ... please

I don't know how

Love me ... please

You don't fit my pictures

Love me ... please.

Copyright © 9/20/97 Erica Goodstone, Ph.D.

Love Is A Gift

Love is a gift, given to us by our Creator. We do not have to work to become worthy of love. **We ARE love.** Our spirit is pure love. No matter what the circumstances of our birth, God intended us to be here. Otherwise, we would not exist. A wonderful poster says, "God Don't Make No Mistakes!" Believe it!

Nothing is more powerful and wonderful than love. What could be more empowering than a supportive mother's love, more endearing than a cooing baby's love, more exciting than being wrapped in the arms of a partner's passionate love, more comforting than a favorite pet's accepting love? What could be more sustaining and healing than believing in God's love and living every moment in a state of self-love?

Love Me … Please, the first book in a four part series, leads us on a path toward loving … truly loving, from the center of our being. Love is the ultimate aphrodisiac. Love is patient, kind, unyielding, enduring and steadfast. Love overcomes all obstacles. But what most of us have called love, our human concepts and human attempts at love, with its sense of limited supply, ownership, and "what's in it for me" attitude, is filled with illusion, self-consciousness, insecurity, doubt and emotional upheaval. True love, unconditional love, a higher state of love, is limitless, boundless, and the ultimate creative power of the universe.

This book is meant for lovers, people who love, people who want to love, people who have loved, and people who want to love again. You will not find simplistic answers and easy to follow formulas for creating love. You will have to look deep into your own consciousness – your thoughts, beliefs, attitudes, memories and dreams – to find the love, the fullest love, that you can bring into your life. And you will be reminded, over and over, to bring that love back to your own self so that you can fully share your loving self with others.

****

LOVE ME ... PLEASE

*"Circumcise therefore the foreskin of your heart,
and be no more stiffnecked."*

Deuteronomy 10:16, King James Version

Love is all there is. Love teaches. Love heals. Sometimes love hurts. You cannot will your self to love. You cannot will another to love you. Love is a feeling, a sensation, and an emotion. When you love, your emotional responses are heightened. You feel deep sorrow, intense anger, and even rage. You also feel exquisite pleasure and the emotional comfort of intimate contact. When you love, you experience the joy and wonder of being fully alive. In this book and this first chapter, you reflect upon love in your life: what you believe about love, how you have loved your self and others, how you have been loved, what you expect from love, and how you can create more love in your life.

LOVE ME ... PLEASE

Love Me ... Please

Love me…please
I am here
Right in front of you
Can you see me?
Do you know who I am?
I am just like you
Really, believe me
It's true

Don't be fooled by me
My outer appearance
Is just a show
I've covered myself
In delicate wraps
Of skin-filled matter
But I am still here
Underneath

I am…
Look deeply
In my eyes
You will find
Yourself
Really
No kidding
I'm your mirror

Copyright © 2009, Revised 2023   Love Me … Please   DrEricaGoodstone.com

Polish my surface
I'll shine for you
Don't cloud my vision
You'll only block
Your own sight
Listen to me speak
You will hear
Your self talk

We belong together
Don't leave me alone
I'm hungry - feed me
I'm thirsty - let me drink
Don't turn away from me
Where else is there
For you to go?
We're here together

Now?
Why?
Let's find out
Let's share ourselves
Expand our views
Teach each other
What we need
To know

Let's love each other
For being here
That's all
Just for being
For existing
We're here
Together
Now

Don't you get it?
The cosmic joke
Ha, ha!
And we keep trying
To run away
From what?
From whom?
From love?

Loving being
Let me rest
In the power
Of your presence
Love me
Now
And always
Please!

Copyright © 9/20/97 Erica Goodstone, Ph.D.

THE GIFT OF LOVE

LOVE ME ... PLEASE

CHAPTER 1

THE GIFT OF LOVE

The Gift Of Love

I have given you
The gift of love
My love
In my way
What have you done
With my love?

Have you welcomed me
Into your heart?
Have you heard
My silent song?
Do you want
To play and know me?

Or- - -

Would you rather
Remain stuck
In your illusion
Of who
You think
I am?

Would you rather
Be right
And close your heart
Than forgive me
For being less
Than you expect?

How can I help you
Overcome your fear
Of loving me so deeply
That you will be
Swallowed up by me
And disappear?

What would it take
For you and I
To open our hearts
And keep them open
Through all the anguish
Of becoming real?

Let's take that first step
Now
See with our eyes
Hear with our ears
And Listen
With our hearts.

Copyright © Erica Goodstone, Ph.D. 4/10/99

Love Is All There Is

Love is a gift, given to us by our Creator. We do not have to work hard to become worthy of love. We are love. Our spirit is pure love. No matter what the circumstances of our birth, God intended us to be here. Otherwise, we would not exist. But you and I do exist. A wonderful poster I have seen says, "God Don't Make No Mistakes!" Believe it!

Each of us was granted life for a reason. There is wisdom in our cells. Our mother's egg connected with our father's approaching sperm. This was not an accident! Our birth was a gift of the Divine. Our birth was a gift of love to humanity, to this planet and beyond.

Who we are is our gift of love. Each of us has an equally important right to be here, to love and be loved. Love is all there is. When we reach the end of our life, as our death is approaching and we review our life, we will probably not think about the money we have earned, the careers we have created, or our favorite automobile. What we will recall, regret, or grieve about is the way we have loved and whether or not we have enjoyed living. As we feel our life slipping away, how we have loved and lived is all that really matters.

When I was 20, in my senior year of college, my father, Morris had a stroke, became progressively more ill, and passed on. All I wanted to do was run away, to escape from feeling the sadness, confusion, fear and loss. Twenty-eight years later, when my mother was dying, I stayed by her side, day and night, throughout her last few days. All I felt was the enduring quality of love and the loss of this precious human life, my mother, Muriel.

We don't need to wait for devastating loss or impending death to feel the love that has always been inside of us. **This is the reawakening.** Regardless of the loss or pain we have endured, in every moment of our life, we can choose to close our heart or open our heart to love.

Love And Intimacy Are Healing

Dean Ornish, M.D. (*Love and Survival,* 1997)) says that without love, connection, and intimacy, we are more likely to suffer and become ill. Without love, we do not thrive. Without love, we seem to just go through the motions of daily life, devoid of pleasure and excitement.

Although love creates the most profound feelings of peace and joy, most of us have not learned how to truly love our self or another. Relationships become a place to suffer. Having suffered once too often, many of us have actually given up on love.

Betty's Husband Leaves

"It's too painful to let anybody get close. I would be devastated if they left. I just can't risk it anymore." These are the words of Betty, a client who was divorced from the man of her dreams and who now appears to have given up on love.

When Betty was a young child, her father moved out of the house, visiting only on birthdays and holidays, when he would arrive loaded down with gifts in beautiful boxes. Betty has been spending the rest of her life searching for the love she never received from her father. She has always expected the man in her life to provide boxes of beautiful gifts just for her, all the time, every moment.

Her husband, Alan, could not compete with the bigger than life image she had of her hapless father. Betty demanded constant, and sometimes impossible, proof that Alan loved her. No matter how much he gave, it was never enough. Finally, Alan gave up and left. Just as her mother had lived without a man since her husband deserted her thirty years earlier, Betty was prepared to spend the rest of her life alone.

Just as we naturally learn a language in the first few years of life, so too, we learn how to love in our earliest years. Synapses and pathways in the brain (as well as intricate chemical reactions that release neuropeptides to receptor cites throughout the body), develop at birth or perhaps even earlier, while we are still growing in our mother's womb. Sensual stimulation, including eye contact, sounds, touch, and mirroring of who we are, in our earliest years, helps these pathways to develop and the neuropeptides to spread. Not receiving that early attention and recognition, our pathways may remain underdeveloped and our chemical responses dulled. We may spend the rest of our life seeking, but not quite getting enough, acceptance and approval from others. Being on the receiving end of too much stimulation, we may develop lifelong states of anxiety, fear, or continually stressful guardedness and a fear of being overwhelmed by what appears to be too much emotional or physical closeness.

Intimacy Is Not For The Faint Of Heart

David Schnarch, Ph.D, (*Passionate Marriage*, **1997**) describes the way many married couples dance between feeling alienated and emotionally distant and feeling pressured and smothered. He devotes an entire chapter to the warning concept "Intimacy is Not for the Faint of Heart." According to Schnarch, intimacy in long-term marriage may require validating our self rather than expecting to receive the mirroring, acceptance and validation from a partner. How we have been loved has a profound effect upon our ability to validate our self and share our love with others.

My doctoral dissertation, based upon the theories developed by psychologist and researcher, Dr. Margaret Mahler, studied the overpowering and conflicting emotions of separation anxiety, intense ambivalence, and anxiety about marriage, residual emotions from our earliest bonding experiences, that can easily interfere with our ability to sustain satisfying love relationships.

Separation – Individuation

Dr. Margaret Mahler (*The Psychological Birth of the Human Infant, 1975*)) observed infants' behavioral and emotional responses, during their first three years of life, to their mother's bonding behavior. She concluded that all children go through a *separation-individuation* process that is strongly influenced by the type of mothering the child receives.

According to Mahler, the infant's first month of life is non-relational. The infant mostly sleeps, awakening only to satisfy hunger, elimination, or other physiological needs. From the second to 18th month, the *symbiosis* stage, an infant is vaguely aware of mother as a source of getting basic needs met, but there is no sense of boundary between infant and mother.

The *separation-individuation* phase, from around the fifth month to 3 years of age, begins with experimentation. Recognizing mother as a separate being, a child discovers his or her own body parts and develops a body image. Early behaviors include pulling mother's hair, ears or nose, putting food into mother's mouth, or the infant straining his or her body away from mother to have a better look at her. From about 7 to 8 months, the infant compares mother to other people. Responding to unfamiliar people with *stranger anxiety*, the child clings to mother and gradually begins to leave mother's side to explore the world. Not ready to go out into the world alone, the child returns often to mother for comfort and *emotional refueling.* With proper mirroring and acceptance from mother, a child begins to individuate, gradually separating, creating boundaries and distance, while still remaining close to mother.

From about 18-24 months and beyond, the ***Rapprochement Crisis*** is said to occur. During this phase, recognizing both parents as separate individuals, a child realizes he or she must cope alone as a small and helpless person. With parents' continual acceptance, love, and encouragement to explore the world, a child learns that separating from a loved one is not the same as losing that person's love. A child who is stifled, held back, or pushed out on his or her own too soon without the emotional support of either parent, will probably grow up with *intense ambivalence* about intimacy. As an adult, he or she may either fear the *separation anxiety* that would result from being abandoned or the *merger anxiety* that would result from being stifled and overwhelmed by another in the process of becoming close. During this rapprochement phase, a child develops, or fails to develop, empathy for others.

The final phase, ***Individuality and Object Constancy,*** is crucial for the creation of mature, satisfying, and egalitarian, love relationships in adult life.

This is the ability to accept both the good and bad qualities in oneself, mother, father, and others. Without a clear sense of individuality or an inability to retain a constant sense of the other person, we will alternate between closeness and distance, creating emotional ups and downs with our most intimate partners.

Good Enough Mothering and Fathering

If we have had *good enough mothering*, a term coined by noted psychologist Winnicott, as well as **good enough fathering,** we may be able to overcome our dependency needs, differentiate from our intimate partners, and validate our own self. If we have not received good enough loving as a child, we will probably spend the rest of our life searching for the love and acceptance we never had. Because we have not learned to trust, we will probably tend to push others away, keeping them at a safe distance, afraid to show how much we need them. It is hard for even the most caring and patient partner to continually support someone who distrusts and feels unloved.

Even if we have had very poor mothering and fathering, painful, neglectful or downright abusive beginnings, we **do have the ability to**

overcome our past, create new pathways in our brain, differentiate as adults, and create intimacy in our life. Intense therapeutic work and powerfully intimate love relationships can assist us to overcome early childhood deficiencies, but nothing can totally erase what has happened, or not happened, in our life. The memories remain. We have to allow our self to feel and express all of our emotions, even the most painful, to reach a point of being able to accept the truth about what is.

Emotions Signal Unmet Needs

Our emotions are signals to us that we have unmet needs. Often we seek to satisfy certain needs while totally ignoring others. For example, one of our needs may be to nurture others. In even the most abusive relationship, we may be able to satisfy that need. But we may be ignoring two equally important needs, the need to nurture our self and the need to be nurtured by another. It is essential to understand our own needs and whether our emotions are a response to our current situation or to an unresolved situation from the distant past.

We often project onto those we love the power to permanently satisfy or deny our unfulfilled childhood needs. During our bouts of lovesickness and despair or unrealistic demands and expectations, we do not realize that this other person is just another human being. We forget that this person was also once a child and may also be harboring some unresolved and unmet childhood needs.

Many of us, men and women alike, give our self away in an attempt to please another. Some of us, on the other hand, put our efforts into influencing, convincing, manipulating, and controlling others to do things the way we decide they must be done. Either of these approaches has disastrous effects upon relationships, especially long term.
All we can have, if we suppress our own emotions or coerce others into suppressing theirs, is some approximation, some illusion, of our own controlled version of love.

What Are Your Nurturing Needs?

Sit quietly. Close your eyes. Breathe deeply and slowly as you allow your body to relax.

Now, reflect upon your most significant relationships, past and present. Do you tend to nurture and validate yourself? Do you tend to nurture and validate others? Open to a new page in your journal and answer the following questions:

In my relationships, in what way do I tend to:

* *ignore my own needs to please others?*
* *make unfair demands on others to please myself?*
* *give more than my share so the other person will need me and not leave?*
* *attempt to keep others off-balance and disempowered, by controlling them with words, money, or unpredictable behaviors?*
* *allow others to control, unbalance and disempower me?*
* *refuse to give to others what they desire, ask for, or say they need?*
* *allow others to deny me what I desire, ask for, or say I need?*
* *usually express my own feelings and ask for what I want?*
* *allow others to express their own feelings and ask for what they want?*

Reflect upon your responses to the previous questions. Decide now:

- *Is this the way I want to be with others?*
- *Is there something more I can do to nurture and validate myself?*

Copyright © 2009, Revised 2023   *Love Me … Please*   DrEricaGoodstone.com

- *Is there a way I can communicate my needs more effectively to others?*
- *Can I can allow others to express their needs without suppressing my own?*

Learning how to love can be difficult. We have to give up the narcissistic belief that we are entitled to immediate gratification of our own needs at the expense of others. We have to let go of our desire to control people and situations. Love involves more than giving and receiving. **When we love, we allow others to exist.** We allow others to be themselves, to strive for their own goals, even if their goals sometimes directly interfere with our own needs and desires.

Research at the Institute of Heartmath indicates that our heart has an intricate electrochemical circuitry that connects directly with our brain. When we feel upsetting emotions, our heart rhythms become uneven and send jumbled information. We are unable to think clearly. Feeling love, we can literally activate coherent heart rhythms and send coherent messages to our brain, leading to emotional well-being and mental clarity.

When we love, there is a rippling effect. Each person who receives our love has more love energy to share with others. Imagine what a world this would be if everyone loved freely, instead of reserving it for only a precious few valued loved ones.

Most of us misunderstand love. We believe that love means loving others regardless of the effect upon our self. Or, we believe we must love our self at the expense of others. Love often requires strength, discipline, and making appropriate choices. Sometimes we must place our own needs on hold while we serve another. At other times we must care for our self first, as in the airplane instructions to put on your own oxygen mask first before helping others.

How Have You Loved?

Looking back at your life, what might you discover about the way you have loved and how you have received love from others? You do not have to wait until you have only a few months, days or moments left to live. You can examine and review your life right here, right now, with the remainder of your life stretching out in front of you.

As you answer the following questions, pay attention to your thoughts, emotions, and bodily sensations. Open your journal to a new page or keep a sheet of paper and pen ready. Sit quietly in a comfortable position. Take a few easy, slow, deep breaths. Relax.

Think about all the people you have loved - family, friends and romantic partners. Select one significant person you have loved. Remember, you can repeat this exercise over and over, focusing on a different person each time, if you choose. Now, answer the following questions about your relationship with one significant person.

How have I shown my love?

How have this person shown love to me?

How have I received their love?

How have they received my love?

How could I have loved them better?

How could they have loved me better?

How could I have loved myself better?

It is often easy to love another when they respond to us in the way we believe is appropriate. But what happens when another person's response is not at all what we feel we deserve, desire or expect? What if someone we love ignores, demeans, invalidates, or outright rejects us?

Not being loved by a particular person does not, by any means, indicate that we are unlovable. Another person's particular needs and desires may not be fulfilled by receiving the gift of our love. All we can do is offer our love and appreciate whatever comes back to us. **We simply cannot please everyone.** In another situation with another person whose needs match our own more closely, we may be accepted and loved exactly the way we are.

Some of us have found that when we loved in the past, the person we loved did not reciprocate by loving us back in the same way with the same intensity. Feelings of abandonment, loss and devastation may have caused us to suppress our emotions and try to protect our self from ever hurting that much again. We begin to behave in unpredictable ways. The result of suppressing our emotions is often misunderstanding, distancing, and hurt feelings. When people disappoint or disagree with us, we may unexpectedly explode in a burst of rage or break down in tears. With self-awareness, self-acceptance, and understanding of the human condition, we can overcome even the most painful loss, rejection or abuse.

How Do You Love Others When You Feel Unloved?

Close your eyes. Sit quietly. Breathe deeply and allow your body to relax.

Remember a time when you loved someone who did not behave lovingly toward you.

Ask yourself the following questions:

What did this person say or do?

How did I respond to this person's words or actions?

How might I have responded if I felt loved no matter what this person said or did?

Was my response and behavior loving toward this person?

Was my response and behavior loving toward my self?

Now, go back to that situation and imagine what would have happened if you had felt totally secure, if you knew with total certainty that you are a worthwhile, lovable person, that your self-worth does not depend in any way upon this person's responses toward you.

Repeat this exercise as often as you like, recalling incidents with different people you have loved.

It is truly impossible to love another person if we do not love our self. Yes, we can feel the stirring of emotions. We can feel lust, desire, even longing. But love is much more complex and inclusive. Love also involves acceptance, forgiveness, and freedom. When we truly love, from the depth of our being, we allow the other person freedom to be who they are, even if we wish they were different.

How Have You Loved Yourself?

Sit quietly. Close your eyes. Breathe deeply and easily. Allow your body to relax.

Ask yourself the following questions:

In what ways do I show love and appreciation toward myself?

Is there anything I find impossible to love about myself?

What would have to change for me to be able to love myself fully?

Through loving and being loved, we know we exist. The opposite of love is not hate. The opposite of love is indifference. Painful as it is to be mistreated or even abused, it may be even more damaging and life threatening to be ignored. Being disregarded tells us we don't count and we do not affect the world around us. Studies have shown that infants who do not receive attention, stimulation, love, and touch, become increasingly despondent, depressed, withdrawn, and eventually die. Even if basic needs for food, water, clothing, and shelter are provided, they do not thrive. As adults, we continue to need to feel loved and to share our love with others. Loving and caring for another person (a child, an adult, even a pet) can be more healing than feeling loved by someone else.

I Love, I Hate

If we do not know what we love or hate, what we want, enjoy, desire, or fear, we cannot know love and we cannot truly love another.

Divide a piece of paper into 3 vertical columns. Put the following words at the top of each column: **I Love / I Hate / I Feel Neutral.** Write at least (20) twenty words or phrases in each column. Notice in which column you have written the most and which column the least words or phrases. As you begin to discover what you truly love, hate, and feel indifferent about, you can return to this page to add and delete words and phrases.

Beliefs

Many of us behave and respond the way we think will be accepted by others, rather than expressing what we truly want and feel in the moment. We may develop self-protecting beliefs that keep us safe and distant from others and perpetuate our inability to recognize and accept love, even when it is right in front of us.

Here are some common beliefs that prevent us from getting close to others.

"If I tell people how I feel, they will humiliate me or abandon me."

"If I tell the truth about someone abusing me, I am hurting someone else."

"I must do everything perfectly in order to be liked and accepted by others.

"If I don't have control in any situation, others will try to hurt me."

"I must be young and fit and beautiful to be desired and loved."

"If I let someone get close and they leave me, I will be devastated and could die."

"If I the person I love rejects me or leaves me, I will never find love again."

"If people disapprove of me, it means something is wrong with me."

"It is safer for me to stay with people and activities that are familiar."

"A good man, lover, husband, father, son, brother should ...."

"A good woman, lover, wife, mother, daughter, sister should ...."

"Sexual desire cannot last even in the best of relationships."

Unfortunately, there may be some truth in some of these statements. We have all had the experience of telling someone how we felt only to be misunderstood, rejected, humiliated or abandoned afterward. Yes, there are some people who will only like us if we do things perfectly, exactly the way they expect. Sometimes if we let others have control they may attempt to hurt us. At times we are temporarily devastated by the loss of another person's love. Yes, some people will not love and desire us if we don't fit their physical ideal. And sexual desire often does not last in long-term relationships. In some situations, with some people, some of the time, we will not be loved the way we want no matter what we say or do. But that does not mean we are unlovable and it does indicate we will never find a person to reciprocate our loving feelings. Our experiences in the world help to create our beliefs. What we believe helps to shape our world.

I Believe

Sit quietly and take a slow deep breath. Allow your body to relax. Open to a new page in your journal. Write each of the following statements at the top of a separate page. Contemplate the first statement for a moment, then close your eyes briefly. Open your eyes and immediately write what you believe about that statement. Repeat this process until you have written your initial beliefs about each statement.

* *I believe ... about love and relationships*
* *I believe ... about touching and being touched*
* *I believe ... about sensuality and sexuality*
* *I believe... about healing*
* *I believe ... about spirituality, a higher power, and God*

Reread your entire list of beliefs and then answer the following three questions:

How have my beliefs affected the way I feel about myself?

Copyright © 2009, Revised 2023   *Love Me ... Please*   DrEricaGoodstone.com

How have my beliefs affected what I dream about and strive to accomplish?

How have events, experiences, and specific people influenced my beliefs?

For the next few days, notice in what ways your life seems to conform to your beliefs. As you complete the exercises in this book, you may be surprised to see that your beliefs gradually change, that they are not as firm and true as you originally thought. Reread your list of beliefs at least once every week. Cross out, revise, and add to your list of beliefs as your life circumstances and your depth of understanding shifts. As you reread your list, you may want to add additional categories, listing your beliefs about such important aspects of life as creativity, money, aging, illness, parents, and children.

Conflicting Beliefs

As you review your list of beliefs, you may be surprised to discover that you hold two or more conflicting beliefs about the same aspect of your life. Harbouring conflicting beliefs can easily interfere with getting what you truly want to have in your life.

For example, if you are a woman who wants a relationship, you may believe, *"A woman must look attractive and sexy to be loved by a man."*

As a woman you may also believe, *"Men use, abuse and leave women who look attractive and sexy."*

A third belief of yours, as a woman, might be, *"I must be strong and never let a man use, abuse and leave me."*

If you are a man who wants a relationship, you may believe, *"A man must always be in control and never reveal his insecurities to be loved by a woman."*

As a man you may also believe, *"Women use, abuse and leave men who are not in control and reveal their insecurities."*

A third belief of yours, as a man, might be, *"I must be strong and never let a woman use, abuse and leave me"*

Given those three beliefs, how might you, as a woman, behave with men?

Given those three beliefs, how might you, as a man, behave with women?

Changing Beliefs

Believing is receiving. Change our beliefs and miracles happen. But how do we change beliefs that developed so long ago and seem so real and true to us? **By feeling our feelings, expressing our emotions, and recreating the story of our life.** We cannot change our beliefs with our mind. Beliefs change through bodily experience. Through our bodies, we feel sensations and express our emotions.

Love is an emotion. Hate is an emotion. Anguish is an emotion. Humans are capable of a wide range of emotions, but most of us have not been allowed to freely express many of our basic emotions. When we do regularly feel and express our true emotions, we may lose something we really want, we may hurt for the moment, but we will also be able to heal more rapidly. Watch children play. They get hurt. They scream and cry and sulk and pout and whine. Suddenly they get distracted. Once again they are playing and giggling as if nothing has happened. Let's become like children in our emotional expression.

How Do I Express My Emotions?

Sit quietly. Close your eyes. Breathe deeply and slowly. Allow your body to relax. Open to a new page in your journal. Contemplate each of the following questions, one at a time, and write your immediate response to each one. After reading each question, briefly close your eyes, contemplate your response, open your eyes, and immediately write your answwers. Do not stop to think or censor your responses.

While growing up, what emotions was I allowed to feel and express?

    With whom?

    In what situations?

While growing up, what emotions was I taught to hide, suppress, or deny?

    With whom?

    In what situations?

How did others respond to me when I showed unacceptable emotions?

As an adult and in recent years, what emotions have I allowed myself to feel and express?

    With whom?

    In what situations?

How have I responded when another person expressed emotions I have not allowed myself to feel or express?

How have others responded to me when I expressed emotions that were previously unacceptable for me to feel and express?

Many of us are afraid we will be punished and rejected if we express our true feelings. Or we fear that uncontrollable and overpowering emotions will come flooding out and we will have an emotional breakdown. We may even be afraid, if we express what we truly feel, our world as we know it will collapse and we will no longer exist.

Research reveals that keeping our emotions locked inside, not expressing our true feelings, can and does make us sick. Such diseases as cancer, arthritis, asthma, high blood pressure, skin rashes, and heart disease can be exacerbated by holding feelings inside. Traditional Chinese medicine associates blocked or weakened organ meridians, such as heart, lungs and large intestine, with specific emotions. Of course, emotions are not the only cause of illness. A healthy life requires balanced living: adequate nutrition, exercise, sleep, rest, stress management, social and spiritual connection. In a later chapter, we will revisit our body in greater detail, but for now, let's take a look at the ways we have loved, nurtured, or ignored our emotional needs.

Each of us has a unique gift to share with the world. We were born into this body at this time for a reason. We may not know the reason, but we do have a purpose for being here. If we cover up our feelings and deny our natural way of being, how can we discover our life's purpose?

We have the power to change our life, to create more of what we want and less of what we don't want. We can begin by telling our self the full truth about where we are in this process, right here, right now. We can review and evaluate the experiences of our upbringing and early childhood. We can discover what we believe was nurturing, non-nurturing, abusive or neglectful. Developing the capacity to create intimate and loving relationships with others requires that we understand and accept our own ability to give and receive love.

What Is My Loving Potential?

Close your eyes. Breathe deeply and quietly. Allow your body to relax. Reflect upon the following question:

How loving am I with the people in my life?

Open to a new page in your journal. Make a list of your current closest friends, lovers, family members, colleagues or anyone with whom you've been spending time lately.

For each person, answer the following questions.

Why am I choosing to be with this person?

What pleases or displeases me about him or her?

What does he or she offer or provide for me?

What do I offer or provide for him or her?

How do I show, hide or disguise my love and other feelings?

Only when we have faced the dark side of our own soul, can we relinquish our demand for approval, acceptance and love from others. At that point, we may be ready to forgive our human mothers and fathers and all those who have hurt, ignored, or disappointed us, for their human frailties, for having given us less than our optimal doses of love, acceptance, and even discipline and boundaries.

Letter to My Birth Mother or

Earliest Caretaker

Write a letter to your birth mother or your earliest caretaker, whoever was most significant to you, the one who sometimes, frequently, or rarely, showed you love and affection, the one who sometimes neglected, disregarded, or hurt you. Express your feelings of disappointment, sadness, rejection, loss, yes, even bitterness, anger and rage. Bang a pillow and scream into it if you must. If you also have some wonderful feelings, then thank your mother for whatever you do appreciate. Hug the pillow if you please.

The Mother of My Dreams

After you have completed this letter, close your eyes and imagine being taken in, nurtured, loved and cared for by the mother of your dreams. Imagine being filled up with a sense that you truly count, you are special, good, and you deserve to be loved and to receive all the good things that life has to offer. Remain connected to this place inside where you feel full and you know you are loved, cared for, and pleased with your life. Coming from that internal place of self-acceptance and self-love, express your true disappointment with and then appreciation, even the smallest amount, for your birth mother or primary caretaker, for who she was, how she raised you, and how you were treated by her.

Letter to My Birth Father or Earliest Father Figure

Write a letter to your birth father or earliest father figure, the one who sometimes, frequently or rarely, showed you love and affection, the one who sometimes neglected, disregarded, or hurt you. Express your feelings of disappointment, sadness, rejection, loss, yes, even bitterness, anger and rage. Bang a pillow and scream into it if you must. If you also have some wonderful feelings, then thank your father for what you do appreciate. Hug the pillow if you please.

The Father of My Dreams

After you have completed this letter, close your eyes and imagine being taken in, protected, loved and cared for by the father of your dreams.

Imagine being filled up with a sense that you truly count, you are special, strong, good, and you deserve to be protected and loved and to receive all the good things that life has to offer. Remain connected to this place inside where you feel full and you know you are loved, cared for, and pleased with your life. Coming from that internal place of self-acceptance and self-love, now express your true disappointment with and then your appreciation, even the smallest amount, for your birth father or primary father figure for who he was, how he raised you, and how you were treated by him.

What Are Your Rules For Loving?

Reread your list of beliefs. Select those 5-10 loving beliefs that seem to rule your life.

On a new page, write: **My Rules For Loving.** Your life is unfolding in accordance with your rules for loving. Change your rules and you change your life.

Many years ago, there was a wonderful TV program, *This Is Your Life.* Each week, a celebrity would be invited for a full life review. Relatives, friends and lovers that had not been seen for many years miraculously appeared. Private fears, insecurities, and childhood problems were revealed and even laughed about. Finally, the invited relatives and friends gathered around to acknowledge and exchange hugs and kisses with the celebrity. At the end of the show, the book was closed. That celebrity's current life story was complete.

This Is Your Life

Join me on a journey back into your distant past. Have your journal ready and opened to a new page. Together we will uncover some early thoughts and experiences, those that helped to form your current beliefs and rules for living.

Sit quietly for a few moments. Breathe slowly, softly and easily.

Allow your mind to wander back along the years to your earliest memories of life.

Recall the words and feelings expressed by your mother, father or other early caretakers about love, touch, healing, spirituality, God, sensuality and sexuality.

Allow your mind to recollect how your beliefs and rules for living were created and developed.

What Are Your Rules for Loving?

Open your eyes and write about your own rules for loving. Write whatever thoughts fill your mind. Write in short phrases, outline form, sentences, or brief paragraphs. Just write and write and write until your mind begins to quiet down, the thoughts slowly dissipate, and you know you are finished for now.

The Eraser Game

Read what you have written about your rules for loving.

Now, reread your long list of Beliefs.

Reread your short list of My Rules for Loving.

Take a red pen and draw a thin line through any beliefs or rules that will not assist you at this point in your life to attain your goals and live your dreams.

This is your life. How do you choose to live it? What rules do you really want to follow? What beliefs and rules will lead you to the promised land, to fulfillment of your dreams and your life's purpose.

Copyright © 2009, Revised 2023   *Love Me ... Please*   DrEricaGoodstone.com

Your New Rules for Creative Loving

On a new page, rewrite your list of rules for loving, retaining only those items that were not crossed out. Add any additional rules for loving that you know will support your goals and dreams, what you want to create in your life. These are your new, expanded, uplifting **rules for creative living.** For example:

"When I speak my truth, others listen."

"Love and respect are part of my life."

"It is fun and exciting to try something new, to learn something I don't already know."

"It is okay for me to make mistakes. I can study, take lessons, practice and improve and become much more skillful than I am now."

Keep an ongoing, expanding list of these uplifting, broadening, expansive, loving, and flexible beliefs and rules for living. Read spiritual and positive books. Add to this list review the list at least once every week, and cross out any rules beliefs that no longer serve you.

Copyright © 2009, Revised 2023   *Love Me ... Please*   DrEricaGoodstone.com

It is not the events in our life that count. It is the way we interpret events and how we choose to live afterwards. Nelson Mandella, a political prisoner in Africa for many years, emerged from his prison ordeal to become the Prime Minister of South Africa! Victor Frankl and Elie Weisel, having suffered unimaginable abuse and indignity for years in concentration camps. Nelson Mandela spent many years incarcerated in Africa due to racial prejudice and political chastisement. These are people who did not bask in their "poor me suffering mentality." Instead, they dedicated the rest of their lives to recording their experiences and teaching others to value their own internal lives, no matter what is happening externally.

Each of us has the potential to be or become almost anything we can imagine. The most important ingredient is belief in what's possible, not what appears to be possible, but what **is** possible. Every great event began with a few brave individuals who were not afraid to speak their truth and make a difference. You and I can make a difference too.

Very few of us have been totally loved and accepted for who we are. Most of us learned that we must do something, become something, or be something, in order to be loved. Even if you were raised by the most exceptionally loving and secure parents, at times you have probably felt hurt, disappointed, frustrated, or even temporarily abandoned. These experiences, painful as they may have been at the time, caused you to feel your feelings, to have compassion for your self and others and to be open to love.. Part of being a healthy human being is the ability to feel and express your emotions. Feeling your most painful emotions enables you to also feel your most pleasing emotions. When you allow your self to feel and express all of your emotions, you develop a true sense of integrity, an inner knowing of who you are. The next step is to acknowledge, accept and appreciate your self for being who you are.

BE WHO YOU ARE

THE GREATEST GIFT

OF ALL

LOVE ME ... PLEASE

CHAPTER 2

BE WHO YOU ARE...THE GREATEST

GIFT OF ALL

Be Who You Are

Man child of the world
Enfold me
Wrap me in your fatherly arms
Protect my fragile spirit
From the dangers
Of my untamed mind

Child woman of the earth
Hold me
Caress me with your motherly touch
Arouse my tired senses
From my fear
Of life and love

Precious child of God
Your firelight
Enriches me
Ignite the smoldering embers
Of my inner fire
So bright

Shine your love light
On my heart
Watch my firework display
Let me dream about
The power
Of your embrace

Copyright © 8/24/99 Erica Goodstone, Ph.D.

THIS CHAPTER IS ABOUT YOU

- **Who you are**
- **Who you have been told you are**
- **Who you believe you are.**

Nobody in the world can tell you who you are. You have your own DNA, your own fingerprints, your own beliefs, and your own sense of self. The purpose of this chapter is to guide you to uncover and discover more and more about who you are.

When someone asks you, "Who are you"?, what is your immediate response?

- *Do you define yourself by your family roles (wife, husband, girlfriend, boyfriend, mother, father, daughter, or son)?*

- *Do you define yourself by your abilities, skills, hobbies, or favorite leisure activities (golfer, chess player, musician, stamp collector, dancer, nature lover, theatre goer)?*

- *Do you define yourself by your work, profession, or non-profession (teacher, lawyer, secretary, truck driver, actress, unemployed, housewife, physically challenged, welfare recipient)?*

- *Do you define yourself by your personality or life experiences, either positive or negative (honest, reliable, intellectual, difficult, easy-going, hot-tempered, recovering alcoholic, adult child of sexual abuse)?*

- *Do you define yourself by focusing on your physical appearance (facial features, body shape, height, weight, age, attractiveness)?*

- *Do you define yourself by your most common emotions (angry, sad, lonely, happy, sensual, frustrated, self-doubting)?*

- *Do you define and describe yourself in any other unique way?*

Would you have described yourself the same way: Ten years ago? Five years ago? Two months ago? Last week? Yesterday? Earlier today? Think about what life events have changed your self-image in the past? Imagine how your self image might change now if:

- your financial situation drastically changed, if you fell in love with someone new, or lost your current partner

- you completed a new training program or degree, got a new job, gave birth, adopted a child, or became a stepparent, a foster parent or a grandparent

- you injured a body part, gained or lost a lot of weight, or contracted a life-threatening disease?

- you found yourself in a relationship where the only choice seemed to be to either abandon yourself or abandon another?

Your opinion of yourself, who you think you are, shifts according to your life experiences and the people with whom you spend your time.

You Are Unique And Special

No Matter What You Think About Yourself!

Each of us is unique and special. There never was an **Erica Goodstone** before. There never will be an **Erica Goodstone** again. And there never was a **YOU** before. There never will be a **YOU** again. Even if someone shares the same name or if you have an identical twin, nobody has your exact appearance, mannerisms, background, experience, or knowledge. Nobody has your exact fingerprints or your DNA.

You are a unique and special human being. How can anyone else in this entire world tell you how you should think, feel or behave? How does anyone else know what caused you to think, feel or be the way you are? Our body, mind, and all of our senses, are bombarded every single moment of every single day with continuous internal and external stimulation. Each of us responds in our own unique way.

Nobody else can determine how we should be. So, why do we spend so much of our personal resources (time, money, emotions, energy) trying to please others, suppressing our own unique traits, even attempting to become something or someone else? Why do we attempt to hide or deny who we are, change our appearance, behavior, even our beliefs, to please or displease others?

Each of us has a unique gift to share with the world. We were born into this body, with this genetic constitution, in this gender, with these racial features, in this family, in this part of the world. I believe that each of us has a purpose for being here, exactly where we are. In my experience over the years with many clients, if we cover up our feelings and deny our natural way of being, we tend to lose our zest for life, become bitter, resentful, angry, or even chronically depressed. Let's take a look at where we are right now, in a non-judgmental, private, personal way.

As you go through these exercises, you may feel uncomfortable and even emotionally upset. But please be reassured now. At the end of this chapter, we will do some special exercises to help you reshape your past, yourself and get you ready for the future you.

Who Are You?
Let's Take A Deeper Look.

Sit facing a mirror. Breathe deeply, slowly and softly. Observe your face and body carefully. Ask the following questions as you gaze deeply into your own eyes.

Allow the answers to come to you spontaneously. Speak your answers out loud, directly to the face you see in the mirror. Write your responses in your journal or on a plain piece of paper. Do not pause to think about your responses.

The exercise you are about to do will be repeated three times. This is a quick method for gathering information about your self from a very deep source within. You will be asking the same questions in the 1st person (Who

Am I?), 2nd person (Who Are You?), and in the 3rd person (Who is [Your Name]?). For the third part of this exercise, if possible, have a fairly recent photograph of yourself available; a driver's license or work I.D. is okay. Respond immediately with the first answers that occur to you.

Who Am I?

Looking directly into your own eyes in the mirror. Ask yourself and answer in the first person:

Who am I? _____

I am a woman/man who _____

What do I like about me? _____

What do I dislike about me? _____

What do I want to change about me? _____

Who would I like to be? _____

Who am I? _____

Who Are You?

Looking directly into your own eyes in the mirror. Ask yourself and answer in the second person, as if you were talking to a close friend:

*Who are you?*_____

*You are a woman/man who*_____

*What do I like about you?*_____

*What do I dislike about you?*_____

*What do I want to change about you?*_____

*Who would you like to be?*_____

*Who are you?*_____

Who Is [Your Name]?

Sign your full name legibly in your journal or on a piece of paper. If you have a recent photograph of yourself, alternate between looking directly into your own eyes in the photograph and looking at your own signature. If you do not have a photograph, keep your eyes focused on your written signature as you ask yourself and answer the following questions in the third person: (For example, *Who is Erica? Erica is ….*)

Who is [your name] _____

[Your name] is a woman/man who _____

What does [your name] like about herself/himself? _____

What does [your name] dislike about herself/himself? _____

What does [your name] want to change about herself/himself? _____

Who would [your name] like to be? _____

Who is [your name]? _____

Who Have You Been Told You Are?

Sit quietly and close you eyes. Take a few easy, slow, deep breaths. Write your responses to this exercise in your journal.

List the names of people who have expressed opinions about you, positive and negative, accurate and inaccurate, honest and dishonest.

What words have they used to describe you, your appearance, your personality, your emotions, and your behavior?

Continue listing names and their opinions of you until you find you are becoming repetitive and have exhausted most descriptions and opinions that others have expressed about you.

No man or woman is an island. We are energetic, sentient, feeling human beings. We affect and are affected by others. No matter how strong, powerful, independent, cool or indifferent we may appear to be, we are all affected, to a greater extent than many of us care to admit, by the attitudes, opinions and behaviors of others toward us. When we are treated with loving kindness and respect, we usually feel good about our self. When we are disregarded, abused, humiliated, or mistreated, we often feel bad about our self.

How Have Others' Opinions Affected You?

Take a careful look at the way other people's opinions have affected you. Ask yourself the following questions. Write the answers in your journal.

What makes me feel good about myself?

What makes me feel bad about myself?

What makes me believe in myself?

What makes me doubt myself?

What makes me feel most proud?

What makes me feel most ashamed?

You are not the opinions that others have of you. You are more than the way you have been treated. You are even more than your own opinion of yourself. Whoever you have become is a result of a lifetime of experiences plus your own unique way of perceiving life.

By now you have probably discovered that you do not need to judge your own value by the responses, actions or reactions of others. Others always see you through their own filters. No matter who you are or what you do or say, they will probably only see you according to their own projections. You may remind them of someone else, you may say something they like or something else they misinterpret, you may need something they can or cannot give, or they may want something they believe you can or cannot give.

Reading this book and doing the exercises can and will change your life. For most of us, revealing our internal truth is terrifying. However, sharing our deepest thoughts and feelings can be life saving. Studies show that women with breast cancer live longer when they regularly attend a group sharing session. Sharing with others, being listened to, and being heard, without judgement, can lessen our fear. Just knowing we are no longer totally alone, no longer forced to face our problems in the dark, allows us to begin the long, slow journey toward healing.

How Have You Taken a Stand For Yourself?

Sit comfortably. Take a few slow deep breaths and relax. Scan through your life.

- *Remember a time when you gave yourself away, did what another person wanted, without expressing your own needs.*

- *Remember a time when you did not tell the truth and face some difficulty directly.*

- *Remember a time when you persuaded another person to give them self away, to do what you wanted, without expressing their own needs.*

- *Remember a time when you expressed your own needs and took a stand for yourself.*

Playing Roles

I grew up believing that smart women know how to handle men. I knew I wasn't being "smart" with men, but my education had not been complete. I never did learn what smart women knew. I never learned what a smart woman does, what she says, how she behaves, or how she "gets" from her man what it is she wants.

So--- I lived relationships in a role. I behaved the way I thought a smart woman would behave or I did just the opposite to test out the smart woman theory. I placated, pleased, and gave myself away, or I demanded, expected, and complained. No matter how I tried to figure out the way to handle a man, the smart woman way, nothing worked.

What Roles Have You Played?

What roles have you played in your life?

What roles are you currently playing in your life?

Why do you play these roles?

What would happen if you stopped playing these roles?

What stops you from being **who you are**?

Playing a role, even if you have figured out the best way to play it, as I never managed to do, is living an incomplete life. Keeping your true self in hiding perpetuates a state of insecurity and often self-loathing. Being yourself -- blemishes, flaws, insecurities, obsessions, peculiarities and all -- allows you to let down your guard, relax and become intimate with others. Hiding in any way prevents the full experience of intimacy. It may prevent you from feeling devastating emotional setbacks but it will also block your passion.

How Did You Become Who You Are?

List the significant events and people in your life that you believe had the greatest effect upon you (positive or negative), the ones who influenced the way you feel about yourself. Summarize the way you feel about yourself in a short descriptive, exaggerated phrase, e.g., Poor Abandoned Rich Girl, The Town Loser, The Stud, The Prom Queen.

In a moment, you will be asked to draw. Have several pieces of plain white paper and plain or colored pencils ready. Drawing, painting and other forms of creative expression can help us to discover deeper meanings about our life than words can ever explain. The shapes, colors, textures and symbols often reveal our unconscious feelings about life and about who we are. It doesn't matter if you draw stick figures or elegant portraits, your message will be clear. Trust in the wisdom of your body and mind to allow your hands to do the drawing. Whatever you draw offers valuable information about who you are. The people in the drawings do not have to appear realistic. They are merely representing the message you received and internalized.

Your Family At Home

Draw a picture of your apartment or home when you were a very young child.

If it was more than one level, find a way to show that, even with just a straight line.

Locate each person in your family in the part of the house you most remember them being. For example: brother in the tool room, father in the garage, mother in the kitchen or bedroom, you sitting with your brother watching TV in the living room.

Your Family At the Dinner Table

Draw a picture of your family at dinner.

Write at the top of the picture, "**Dinner With [My Family]**"

For example, "Dinner With The Goodstone Family"

Answer the following questions:

Did you all sit around a table together?

Where did each person sit?

Who cooked?

Who cleaned up after?

What was the general theme? For example, *don't make waves; love and acceptance; criticizing, arguing, insulting; intellectual conversation; solving the world's problems; gossiping; food; money; beauty.*

Now, give the picture a title that represents the mood of your family at the dinner table. For example, "The News of The World," "How to Save a Buck."

Copyright © 2009, Revised 2023   *Love Me … Please*   DrEricaGoodstone.com

Your Creative Expression

These exercises are designed to help you remember what it was like for you as a child when you were drawing, painting or sculpting; moving your body, being athletic, or dancing; cooking, sewing or cleaning; inventing, building, repairing, solving mathematical problems or connecting electrical wires; speaking, singing, acting, being a comedian or a clown.

Drawing, Painting and Sculpting

Sit quietly. Breathe deeply and allow yourself to relax. Remember a time, when you were very young, when you were drawing, painting or sculpting.

What responses do you remember receiving from others?

What do you remember being told about the way you draw, paint or sculpt?

Who told you this?

Were you encouraged and guided or discouraged and criticized?

What effect did those words and reactions have upon your ability, confidence, and freedom to draw, paint, sculpt, and express yourself?

Imagine yourself drawing, freely expressing your creative genius. Imagine yourself painting with different mediums (watercolor, oils, pastels). Imagine yourself sculpting a work of art with clay or plaster or chipping away at a piece of marble. Imagine yourself to be a creative genius at work, on the level of the masters (Monet, Picasso, Rembrandt, Michelangelo). In your mind, see the people who guided, taught, encouraged and applauded you and your work. In your mind, see the *people* who criticized, judged, interfered with, blocked, repressed or stopped your creative genius from expression.

Moving Your Body, Dancing and Being Athletic

Remember a time, when you were very young and you were moving, dancing, or participating in an athletic activity. You may have received different responses to the way you moved, danced or about your athletic ability.

What responses do you remember receiving from others?

What do you remember being told about the way you move, dance, or your athletic ability?

What do you remember being told about the way men or women should move, dance, or do athletic activities?

What do you remember being told about your athletic ability, flexibility, strength, coordinate, endurance?

Who told you this?

Were you encouraged and guided or discouraged and criticized?

What effect did those words and reactions have upon your ability, confidence, and

freedom to move, dance, participate and succeed in sports, and express yourself?

Imagine yourself moving and dancing. Imagine yourself to be a creative genius at work, on the level of the masters (Rudolph Nureyev, Martha Graham, Magic Johnson, Roger Federer). Draw yourself freely expressing your creative genius. Imagine yourself being athletic in a solo activity (running, swimming, bicycling). Again, imagine yourself to be a superior athlete, at a highly competitive level. Imagine yourself being athletic in a team sport or activity (basketball, volleyball, football, soccer, cheerleading). In your mind, see the people who guided, taught, encouraged and applauded you and your work. In your mind, see the people who criticized, judged, interfered with, blocked, repressed or stopped your creative genius from expression. Now, imagine playing music and dancing around the room. Imagine yourself playing basketball, volleyball, tennis, golf, or whatever sport you may have strong feelings about. If you feel competent or afraid, allow the feelings to emerge. Remember, your feelings are not who you are.

Cooking, Sewing and Cleaning

Remember a time, when you were very young when you were cooking, sewing or cleaning.

What responses do you remember receiving from others?

What do you remember being told about the way you cook, sew or clean?

What do you remember being told about the way men or women cook, sew, or clean?

Who told you this?

Were you encouraged and guided or discouraged and criticized?

What effect did those words and reactions have upon your ability, confidence, and

freedom to cook, sew, clean, and express yourself?

Imagine yourself cooking and sewing. Imagine yourself to be a creative genius at work, on the level of a master chef or master tailor. Imagine yourself freely expressing your creative genius. In your mind, see the people who guided, taught, encouraged and applauded you and your work. In your mind see the people who criticized, judged, interfered with, blocked, repressed or stopped your creative genius from expression.

Now, imagine cooking a delicious gourmet meal. Now, imagine taking a needle and thread and sewing. Now, imagine cleaning your apartment or house. Allow this exercise to bring you deeper into your own feelings. If you feel competent, inappropriate or afraid, allow the feelings to emerge. Remember, your feelings are not who you are.

Inventing, Building, Repairing, Doing Mathematical or Electrical Work

Remember a time, when you were very young when you were inventing, building, repairing, or solving mathematical problems or connecting electrical wires.

What responses do you remember receiving from others?

What do you remember being told about the way you invent, build, repair, or work with electrical wires?

What do you remember being told about the way men or women invent, build, repair, or work with electrical wires?

Who told you this?

Were you encouraged and guided or discouraged and criticized?

What effect did those words and reactions have upon your ability, confidence, and freedom to invent, build, repair, work with electrical wires, and express yourself?

Imagine yourself inventing, building, repairing, solving mathematical problems or connecting electrical wires. Imagine yourself to be a creative genius at work, on the level of a master inventor, builder, mathematician or electrician. In your mind, see the people who guided, taught, encouraged and applauded you and your work. In your mind, see the people who criticized, judged, interfered with, blocked, repressed or stopped your creative genius from expression.

Speaking, Singing, Playing an Instrument, Acting, Being a Comic, Being a Clown

Remember a time, when you were very young when you were speaking, singing, playing a musical instrument, acting, being a comedian or a clown.

What responses do you remember receiving from others?

What do you remember being told about the way you speak, sing, play an instrument, act, tell jokes, or behave like a clown?

What do you remember being told about your ability to speak, sing, play a musical instrument, act, be a comedian or a clown?

What do you remember being told about your right to speak, sing, play a musical Instrument, act, be a comedian or a clown?

What do you remember being told about the way men or women speak, sing, play a musical instrument, act, be a comedian or a clown?

Were you encouraged and guided or discouraged and criticized?

What effect did those words and reactions have upon your ability, confidence, and freedom to speak, sing, play a musical instrument, act, be a comedian or a clown?

Imagine yourself speaking, singing, playing a musical instrument, acting, being a comedian or a clown. Imagine yourself to be a creative genius at work, on the level of a masterful and famous speaker, singer, musician, actor, comedian or clown. Draw yourself freely expressing your creative genius. See the people who guided, taught, encouraged and applauded you and your work. See the people who criticized, judged, interfered with, blocked, repressed or stopped your creative genius from expression. Now, imagine giving a lecture to a large audience. Now, imagine singing a song out loud. Now, imagine playing a musical instrument like a virtuoso. Now imagine being a star, acting in your favorite drama, romance, mystery or comedy. Now imagine yourself being an hilarious comedian. Now, imagine yourself being a famous clown. If you feel competent or afraid, allow the feelings to emerge. Remember, your feelings are not who you are.

Your Creative Expression Collage

You are about to create a collage that represents your creativity and self-expression. Before you begin this exercise, have the following materials ready.

- Different types of magazines (financial, sports, entertainment, hobbies)
- Scotch tape or paste
- Scissors
- Pen, pencil or magic marker
- Large piece of white paper, preferably heavy like cardboard, or several pieces of white paper that you can scotch tape together to make a larger sheet

Now that you've gotten a good sense of who you are, how you feel, how your creative expression has been allowed to develop or how it was discouraged and suppressed, you are ready to begin removing what doesn't really feel like who you are.

Sculpting Yourself

Removing That Which Is Not You

Write each of the questions in this exercise at the top of a separate page in your journal or on a piece of paper. *Who Am I,?, Who Are You,? Who Is [Your Name]?* Sit facing yourself in the mirror. Gaze into your own eyes. Breathe slowly, deeply and softly. Ask yourself the same three questions that you asked at the very beginning of this chapter. Write your answers now in your journal.

Who am I?

Who are you?

Who is [Your name]?

Re-read your three lists.

Cross out any statements that do not belong to you, that do not truly express who you are.

Add any additional statements that reflect who you now think you are.

Who Are You?

Sit facing yourself in the mirror.

Take a few slow, deep, soft breaths.

Gaze into your own eyes in the mirror.

Read aloud the three new lists of statements (*Who am I? Who are you? Who is [your name]?*).

Congratulations! In completing this chapter, you have done some of the most intense and difficult work on yourself that you have probably ever done. You are now becoming more deeply acquainted with who you really are. Before you can connect intimately and truly love another person, it is essential that you know, acknowledge and accept who you are. When you truly allow your authentic self to shine through and you actually are able to appreciate your self for being who you are, you are finally ready to begin the delicate dance of love.

THE DELICATE DANCE OF LOVE

LOVE ME ... PLEASE

CHAPTER 3

THE DELICATE DANCE OF LOVE

The Delicate Dance of Love

In my dreams
I see you
Valient angel
Of the vast blue sky
You sit upon a floating cloud
Waiting for me

In my prayers
I call to you
Courageous voyager
Through uncharted paths
Lead me to my dream
I'll follow

Now you're here
In front of me
Imagined lover
Come to life
Let's walk the path of love
Together

Come with me
To a quiet place
And rest awhile
Our journey has just begun
Take my hand and hold me
In your heart

Let's build a bridge
Stairway to heaven
Let's take those long steps
One by one
See the blossoms all around us
Feel their fragrance in our hearts

Love's sweet journey
Moves us onward
Hearts in sync with nature's flow
Do not fear
Our hearts are open
Do not fear our love is pure

Dancing gently
Toward each other
Moving freely as we meet
Long embrace in cold of winter
Cooling breeze
In summer's heat

First you lead
Through storm and passion
Walking forward toward the light
The path of love continues onward
Hearts on fire
Leading home

Copyright © 8/19/99 Erica Goodstone, Ph.D.

The Delicate Dance of Love

Two people meet. Tingly sensations delight their bodies. Their eyes sparkle at the sight of this wondrous face and body. Each one feels the vibrant pull of ecstatic energy. Their skin moistens with excitement and anticipation. Their ears perk up as each one savors the sound of the other's voice and heartbeat. Their hearts are soft and open. As their lungs expand, their sinuses widen and their throats enlarge. Their noses sense the other's being and retain the sweet smell of imminent pleasure. Their groins ache with desire for love. They breathe like sweet ambrosia the sight and sound and smell of their object of desire.

A line of unseen energy pours between them, holding them still, entranced. Opening their mouths and almost tasting each other's lips, they begin to speak -- tender, gentle, receptive words of admiration, appreciation and unconditional recognition of each other's worth. Even if their words appear harsh, as may be their style, the underlying meaning is clear to both.

And they begin the dance of love....

He fixes his tie (that may not be there) as she pushes back her long flowing hair (that may be closely cropped). The energy in the ethers between them intensifies and spreads beyond. Easing into each other's space, slowly, effortlessly, a force of nature seems to pull them, magnetically, along an electric wire about to explode.

Finally ... they touch, a fleeting touch at the very outer surface of the hairline of their skin. Waves of shock spread throughout their electrified bodies. Hearts aflame, mouths moistening, they have met - - and touched - - at the contact zone of love.

Passionate Hollywood movies and popular romantic novels reveal to us the power of physical attraction and intimate contact. Man meets woman. Man meets man. Woman meets woman. Woman meets woman. Electricity fills the air. This is the beginning of love at the contact zone, a term coined by Laura Perls, wife of the originator of Gestalt Therapy, Fritz Perls. The contact zone is a place of ultimate intimacy, a place where our body, mind and spirit join with another. At the contact zone, there is bare honesty in the moment, without need to pretend, to hide, or to escape. This is a sacred place and time, where our body cells listen, respond and openly receive love. This level of intimacy can occur in any relationship -- with close friends, business associates, acquaintances, family members, as well as and with our most intimate lovers.

Love begins at this point of pure contact, but it does not end here. Loving and learning to love is an ongoing creation. It requires mindfulness, attention, commitment, practice, caring and creativity. The most loving thing we can do for others is to honor them by speaking our truth, gently yet firmly, in the moment, the right moment, as if the hands of our heart could caress their soul as we speak.

None of us is an island unto our self. We affect and are affected by others all the time. This world and the entire universe is based upon relationship, one electron to another, one planet to another, one cell to another, one person to another. No matter how cool, indifferent, isolated or independent any one of us appears to be, we have all been affected by others and we all have our unique affect upon others.

Through our skin and all of our senses, we make contact with the world, we know and become known by others. Our eyes see and we are seen. Our ears listen and our voices are heard. We taste and smell our environment and our scent is experienced by others. Our energy and life force, our thoughts and our body posturing, our subconscious beliefs and attitudes, are seen or felt and responded to by others.

Some of us are currently unable to tolerate the pleasurable sensations of intimate contact. From negative life experiences, we may have become so numbed to sensation that the intensity must be high, even painful, for our mind to allow our body to feel. But all is not lost. Healing is possible in every moment, if we truly desire to create intimate relationships in our life.

If we have received caring and tender love, if our senses have been allowed to feel, explore and connect without interference, then we may easily and often reach that place of pure contact with others. At that intimate place, we understand each other without words. Our body comes alive with passionate desire and sensual pleasure.

In the following exercise, you have an opportunity to allow your mind to create the ideal romantic fantasy that you imagine would bring forth your own sexual and romantic passion. Your mind is powerful. Allow your self to dream, to fantasize, and to imagine the way it could be, if only….

My Romantic Fantasy

You are about to become the director, producer, and leading actor in your own romantic fantasy. Create a cast of characters. Put in as many details as you choose. Place yourself as the leading man or leading woman in your own romantic story. Exaggerate! Think big and beautiful, rich and famous. Celebrate *you* in your own romantic vision. Imagine yourself having and being more than you ever dreamed possible. Not just for the moment; for a lifetime, your lifetime, this lifetime, now. Ask yourself the following questions:

Who is romantically involved with me?

How do I look, feel, behave, and express myself?

What do I experience, receive, or become?

Where do I live, travel, and play?

When do the events happen: daytime, evening, season, and year?

Why have I chosen these people in this romantic fantasy?

How does my romantic vision compare to my current romantic life?

Imagination is the most powerful tool we will ever have in our lives. Nobody can take our imagination away from us -- except -- if **we** allow our own dreams to be denied, suppressed or invalidated. Nothing has ever been achieved without starting in somebody's mind as an idea, a thought, an image or a concept. Imagination has led to every major scientific breakthrough, musical and artistic masterpiece, architectural monument, and even Olympic or World Cup athletic competition.

The lives and physical brains of acknowledged creative geniuses, such as one of the leading scientist of the 20th century, Albert Einstein, have often been examined in the futile attempt to discover a unique physiological reason for such unusual creative ability. Brain researchers have found no physical manifestation of creative genius within the brain, no one location, no unique size or shape or density of brain tissue.

What researchers have discovered about creativity is that it often appears to come as a moment of revelation, a sudden insight, a dream, an image or a symbol. The original idea, the necessary steps to be taken, or the final solution to an ongoing problem have usually not been found by working hard at trying to figure out a solution. It seems to be that we must take the necessary steps to learn what we can learn through our brains and logical abilities. But if we rely solely upon our brains and what appears to be logical in the present moment, we will be unable to create. **Logic and control do not lead to creative solutions.**

We cannot control our imagination but we can allow it to flourish. We can use our imagination to create, first in our mind and eventually in physical reality, the type of love relationships we truly want, not the ones we think we must settle for because of some preconceived idea of who we think we are and what we think is possible.

If we give up our dreams before we allow them to manifest in reality, we lose out on an opportunity to discover our own creative powers. Before attempting to imagine and dream about what we want to manifest, it is important for us to examine our current thoughts. And we need to know what we want. Once we have done the logical thinking and we know what we want, we can sit back, relax, and enjoy the show. We can imagine having it all -- exactly the way we want it to be.

Why Do I Want A Relationship?

Why do you want to have a love relationship?

How do you feel when you are alone and not involved in a love relationship?

What do you hope to experience, to feel, or to have by being romantically involved with another person?

How is a love relationship better than being alone, better than friendship or family?

Is there any other way for you to achieve the same feelings or goals?

No matter how much activity and how many people we use to fill the hours and minutes in our daily life, none of us can escape the ultimate truth. We are, each of us, inescapably alone. We are also, all of us, inescapably connected to each other and to everything around us.

We are born alone. Nobody can be born for us. Even identical twins are born separately. We die alone. Nobody can die for us. Even if others are dying at the exact same moment, each of us will experience our own death.

Since we are ultimately alone, why do we need each other? Why not learn to face our own aloneness now? The answer is simple. We need contact with our environment and with each other to know we are alive, to stay alive, to stimulate our senses, to touch, to heal, and to love and be loved. We require contact with others to know our own self.

People naturally make contact with infants, smiling at them, cooing and googling with contorted faces and sounds, often imitating and mirroring the baby's expressions. Without such contact, infants do not thrive. Foundlings raised in The Crêche, an orphanage in Lebanon in the 1950's, received only minimal sensual stimulation, touch, and human contact. Their intelligence did not develop past an IQ of about 80. However, once Lebanon's laws changed and adoption became legal, infants who were adopted into families before two years of age, were able to re-establish average levels of intelligence. Too little stimulation proved to be equally, or even more, detrimental to emotional and physical development as intense stimulation or actual physical and sexual abuse can be.

Intimacy with another, from infancy onward, allows us to expand all of our senses. We discover sounds, sights, words, images, feelings, and tastes that stimulate us. True intimacy requires sensitivity and kindness. It is not blatant honesty and continual verbal communication. It is not continual, intrusive physical contact. Intimacy allows us a combination of closeness, privacy, and personal space, to think our own thoughts, feel our own feelings, re-establish our own body rhythms, and connect with our own self.

When we are intimate, we are aware of how we affect others and how they affect us. If we are afraid to touch or be touched and our partner grabs us too soon, we may give in, we may even feel pleasure -- for awhile. But sooner or later, as we "come to our senses," reconnect with our own inner self, we will probably pull away to find a safe retreat. Sometimes our body responds and we become physically intimate with another, ignoring the effect upon our emotions. Once the bodily sensations have dissipated, we may be left with confused and painful emotions about having been so physically intimate. This can happen when we become involved sexually with a person we hardly know, when someone that we do know coerces, manipulates, or threatens us into sexual involvement, and even at times within a long term committed love relationship.

With a partner who cares about our feelings, one who allows us the time and space to open up at our own pace, we may gradually begin to reach out to touch and be touched. Together we can tentatively explore more and more sensual and intimate touching.

Problem is, often the person who allows us to take our time, to open up slowly, is also a person who is fearful about becoming intimate. If we are not careful, we may retreat from each other and lose the moment, the possibility of a deeper physical and emotional connection.

Ultimately, a close relationship allows us to become more intimate with our own self. Just as nobody else can be born or die for us, each of us must eventually face our own self and do our own inner work. No relationship or loving romantic partner can save us from having to face our own self. They may delay the process, but in the end, we cannot escape the inevitable.

Before we can become intimate with another person, we need to know what we want, what we believe, what we think about our self, about others, and about relationships. Once we are clear about our own thoughts and our true desires, only then can we begin to create what we truly want.

What Do I Believe About Relationships?

Sit quietly. Breathe deeply and slowly. Open to a new page in your journal. Make a list of what you believe about relationships. Here are some samples, but you can add many of your own ideas and concepts and beliefs.

Relationships are difficult because....

Men/women always ....

Men/women should ....

If I show how I feel ...

I'm too good, too difficult, too set in my ways, too ....

List all those beliefs that you are aware of now and add to the list over time.

What Do You Expect To Receive From A Love Relationship?

How do you expect your partner to behave with you, with others?

What actions do you expect your partner to take for you?

What gifts and material comforts do you expect your partner to provide for you: emotional, physical, mental, social, financial, and spiritual?

Copyright © 2009, Revised 2023 *Love Me … Please* DrEricaGoodstone.com

What do you feel and how do you respond when you did not receive what you expect in a relationship?

What determines whether you stay or break off the relationship?

What Do You Expect To Give To A Love Relationship?

How do you expect yourself to behave with your partner, with others?

What actions do you expect to take for your partner?

What gifts and material comforts do you expect to provide for your partner: emotional, physical, mental, social, financial, and spiritual?

What do you expect your partner would feel and respond if you did not give what he or she expects to receive in a relationship?

What determines whether your partner will stay or break off the relationship?

In the early stages of a relationship, many of us give beyond the call of duty. Some of us will appear to be self-less and unconditionally loving, giving and caring. Sometimes both of us are giving more than our share, but in different areas. One of us may pay the bills while the other gives up freedom of choice and independence. Women often give sex in order to receive love. Men often give gifts of love in order to receive sex.

Sex and love are not up for barter in an intimate relationship. The whole point of being intimate is to reveal ourself to others and in that process become intimately connected to our own self. When we are intimate, there is no place for deception and manipulation. Intimacy is a shared, beautiful, heart-warming, expansive connection between two people who care about each other. Why give the most precious jewels we have, the doorway to our soul, for anything less than intimate connection with someone who loves, accepts, and encourages us to be who we are?

Love Is the Essence of Life

Love is the essence of life. Love inspires us and instills us with confidence. Love provides us with honor and strength, ambition and hope, and the promise of fulfilling our dreams. Love is the answer to any question. Love is also the question.

We love another person for what they represent to us -- wealth, sophistication, beauty, intelligence, comfort or recognition. We love another person who seems to embody a quality we think we are lacking and would like to attain. We love someone for a quality we believe we both have in common. We love someone who lacks an important trait as long as we believe, often erroneously, that we can teach, train, discipline or change that quality because of our love.

We feel love for someone who listens and seems to understand us. Sometimes, we feel love when we are rejected, ignored, misunderstood, frustrated and demeaned. At times, we love someone who does all the "right" things for us. At other times, we love a person who seems to do everything "wrong."

No matter what we do, **all of us need love.** We are born to love. All of our actions can be seen as an expression of love, a rejection of love, a cry for love, or even a screaming for love:

- *Why can't you love me?*

- *Why do you have to love me?*

- *How mean can I be, how much can I hurt, reject, and abandon you, yet still know you will love me and not abandon me?*

- *How good an actor do I have to be to win your love?*

It doesn't matter what you do, what you say, or what you feel at any given moment. In the end, all you are is pure love, forever searching to be loved and accepted.

Copyright © 2009, Revised 2023   *Love Me … Please*   **DrEricaGoodstone.com**

Following the path of love is rarely easy. It is strewn with obstacles and problems. Some of us are easy to love. We look inviting, act friendly, entertain, joke, and touch with gentle abandon. Some of us are distant and aloof, shy and clumsy, arrogant and difficult. Perhaps we keep people at a distance and wonder why we feel alone.

It is usually easy to love someone who pleases us and behaves in a way that we find appropriate. The true test is whether we can maintain our equilibrium and continue loving when the other **does not** offer us what we think we want, need, or desire. The question to ask our self is: *Can I continue loving when love keeps testing my fortitude, pushing my limits of endurance, dipping the scales of my self-esteem?* Only **you** can decide if you have given your very best love to another. Only you can love. Nobody else can do it for you!

In the following exercise, we are beginning the path toward unconditional love. It starts with the simple yet powerful intention to love. We notice how we are loving or not loving in every moment of our day. And we review our day by recalling how we have loved.

Copyright © 2009, Revised 2023 *Love Me … Please* <u>DrEricaGoodstone.com</u>

How Will I Love Today?

Beginning this week

- Practice waking up each morning with the question, *How will I love today?*

- Then, in each moment and every activity throughout the day, ask yourself, *Is this love? Is this the most loving I can be -- **to myself** and to others?*

- As the evening draws to a close, review your day by asking, *How have I loved today? Could I have loved more?*

- Always remember to add: *How have I loved **myself** today? Could I have loved myself more?*

Does the thought of waking up intending to love, spending the day engrossed in love, and going to sleep still pondering love, seem impossible? It's only impossible if you believe it is. Why not try it and see what happens?

Loving does not begin out there. The more our focus is outside our own self, expecting to receive love from others, the more we see lots and lots of evidence that most people are unworthy of our limited, narrowly focused small amount of love.

Learn to focus inside, inside your self, inside your own private thoughts and feelings. Notice the way your mind judges your self and others. Notice when your heart refuses to open. It takes great courage to love another as we get to know them better. It takes even greater courage to love our own self as we come face to face with our own shadow: our own fears, insecurities, weaknesses, inadequacies, failings, and flaws.

Love begins as truth. Truthfully, we look inside our own mind. We gradually release and discard old messages, old feelings, old beliefs, and old conditioning. Truth washes away all deceit, all pretense, and eventually all expectation and emotional pain.

What remains, when all else dissolves, is love. Love is behind all emotion. Love is behind all desire. Love is behind all thought. Lack of love is behind all pain. If we delve deep enough inside and continue long enough, we will always reach love.

Why not reach inside now? Discover the love inside just waiting to be expressed.

Have You Given Up On Love?

Have you given up on love? After years of struggling with difficult and painful relationships, many of us feel like giving up. We may come to the conclusion that sex and passion are a hassle and life is calmer, easier and better without the entanglement of attempting to get close to someone else. If we are confused or have given up, we may have some very good reasons.

Most of us are not taught how to love. Many of us do not know how to give love. We may also have difficulty accepting love. And most of us do not know how to sustain love. We may believe that love comes to those who are entitled to it, those who are young, beautiful, clever, rich, successful, with special abilities, or just born lucky. We may believe we have not yet met the right person. We may believe we were raised in a hopelessly dysfunctional family and because of that we have an inexcusable, reprehensible, and unchangeable personality flaw.

No matter what we believe, somebody out there is waiting to love us. All we need to do is let go of our preconceived ideas and open our heart to love. If we have even the smallest desire to be close to another person, it is vital for us to examine our own patterns: what we think, what we say, and how we respond to others. Emotional, physical, spiritual and sexual reawakening is about discovering the hidden potential in our life and in our relationships, eliminating whatever interferes with our capacity for intimate connection.

Touch, love and intimacy are basic human needs, as necessary as the food we eat and the air we breathe. These should be natural and easy components of our intimate relationships. But for many of us, touch is something to be avoided, love is scary, and intimacy is impossible. Sometimes we are involved with a partner who is fearful of intimate touching. Sometimes, we are the one with touch aversion. Sometimes we have a partner who oversteps our boundaries, ignores our requests for intimate touching, or is unable to let us freely be our self in their presence.

Sometimes, we are with a partner who is verbally demeaning or physically abusive. With a partner whose ability to love is stifled, blocked or mixed with abandonment, hatred and abuse, we are unable to thrive. We begin to close down our natural intuitive and creative abilities. We learn to doubt our own feelings, live with anger, frustration and even rage, and ignore what we want most in our life.

Eventually, we may rebel and begin to develop a sense of strength, resolve and determination to take care of ourself. When we are seriously ready to leave, this difficult partner's sweet, loving, tender side may reappear.

Copyright © 2009, Revised 2023 *Love Me … Please* **DrEricaGoodstone.com**

Whatever our partner has been witholding, he or she may lavish upon us with flamboyant exaggeration. Suddenly we receive those flowers, that anniversary gift, a home cooked meal, or a night of tender sex that we have been requesting for a long time. But once we are back in the relationship, the patterns that created our desire to leave will probably return.

If you currently feel stuck in an emotionally painful relationship that you are unable to leave, you are not alone. The emotional web of intimate relating is often complex. Many of us feel guilty, ashamed, and even humiliated when we find we are confused and unable to make a firm decision. There is no shame in being confused about love. Whatever you avoid confronting will probably continue to plague you. There is nothing in your life you cannot face. Begin to face your life now. Deal with the fears and problems now. Your future life is created by the thoughts and beliefs you develop and the steps you take now.

The Way Out

If you've been struggling with an emotionally difficult relationship, perhaps for years and years, don't despair. **There is a way out!** Begin by taking an objective look at your current relationship situation.

- *Are your needs, desires and dreams being satisfied?*

- *Are you expecting too much or too little from your partner?*

- *Is your partner showing a willingness to meet you halfway?*

- *What could you do together to improve the situation?*

- *Is your sexual relationship the glue that is holding together an otherwise impossible situation?*

- *Is your lack of pleasurable sex together destroying an otherwise good relationship?*

Remember the following four statements about your relationship:

- **I cannot willfully change my partner to be the way I expect.**

- **I cannot control my partner's attitudes, behaviors or responses.**

- **I CAN offer my love without demanding an expected response.**

- **And most of all, I can always LOVE MYSELF.**

LOVE YOURSELF, LOVE YOURSELF, LOVE YOURSELF!

Now, love your partner in a way that allows you to continue loving yourself. Allow the relationship to take its natural course. Reread the above section as often as you like.

DON'T PASS THE ABUSE TEST

This is one test you want to fail, you need to fail. Don't be a winner at the expense of your heart, your self-esteem, and your well-being. Don't be a winner at the expense of your partner's heart, your partner's self-esteem, and your partner's well-being. For each of the following situations, ask yourself:

- *Is this an abusive pattern or was one of us momentarily self-absorbed and accidentally disregarding the other's needs?*
- *How do each of us typically respond?*
- *Do I see any similar patterns in my other intimate, social, or professional relationships currently or in the past?*

RED FLAGS OF ABUSE

- You or your partner regularly arrives very late for appointments with a lame excuse.
- You or your partner cancels plans at the last minute, or forgets and doesn't show up.

- You or your partner's requests and feelings are often ignored.

- You or your partner spends more time with others than alone together.

- You or your partner expresses their own views and interrupts when the other speaks.

- You or your partner flirts with others and labels the other "insecure" or "crazy" if they get upset.

- You or your partner calls when to get some need met -- money, a sympathetic ear -- but has little time to call when the other person expressed a need.

- You or your partner seeks the other's professional expertise -- legal, accounting, counseling, fitness training -- for free.

- You or your partner seems sensitive and caring, but criticizes or attacks when the other is most vulnerable.

These and other similar behaviors are red flags of abuse. Abusive attitudes and behaviors do not magically disappear. If you are currently involved in an abusive relationship, be reassured. You are not alone. You have lots of company. Many of us have been there. In fact, many of us are there right now. Sometimes the abuse goes back and forth. Sometimes it is only one-sided. The red flag is the way you feel whether you remain in a calm and loving state together or if you are both riding an emotional roller coaster.

What Is Sexual Abuse?

You may be one of the lucky people who have never had to deal with physical or sexual abuse. Statistics indicate, however, that as many as one in four women and one in seven men have been sexually abused at some time in their lives. And that is only the number of reported cases.

Sexual abuse comes in many forms. Blatant physical sexual assault is fairly easy to identity and even confront. There's a more subtle form of abuse, often difficult to recognize and label as abuse. One type is physical stimulation that is too intense for the individual's system, such as inappropriate touch and persistent tickling. Visual stimulation can be equally overwhelming, especially for a prepubescent child. For example, a boy is asked to hook up his mother's brassiere, a young girl shares a bath with her naked father, a fully clothed nanny touches a naked child in a sensual way, or a pre-adolescent boy follows his mother into the ladies' locker room, where adult women are coming out of the shower naked.

A form of sexual abuse that is rarely talked about is a subtle form of sensual and emotional manipulation. This is often behavior that is emotionally beneficial to an adult or parent without regard for the potential effect upon the child. A woman who is frustrated in her marriage and makes derogatory comments about men, may affect her son's ability to accept himself as a man. A girl whose father really wanted a son may literally become the "man" her father always wanted. A girl may become "daddy's girl," a substitute for the wife her daddy is not intimate with. A boy may play the role of husband to a sexually or emotionally unfulfilled mother.

Abuse can also happen verbally. Teasing, suppressing, denying and invalidating another person's appearance, thoughts and emotions can lead to lifelong emotional insecurity that affects the potential for intimate relating. Older brothers and sisters can sometimes traumatize their younger siblings without the parents awareness or protection.

Have you been sexually abused in a subtle or not so subtle way? Go back in time, and attempt to recall the physical, emotional, visual and verbal messages you received.

- *What examples did your relatives and teachers present to you?*
- *Did people in authority allow you to express yourself or be yourself?*

The first step to uncovering and then undoing childhood abuse, no matter how small and insignificant or devastating and overwhelming, is to take an honest look at what actually happened, what you experienced, what you believe about yourself and others as a result, and the long-term effects in your current life.

If you feel that some of your early experiences are now interfering with your current relationships, why not seek professional help? Our feelings and memories are stored within our body cells. Body oriented and somatic psychotherapy can help us to uncover suppressed emotions and understand what interferes with our ability to enjoy pleasurable and intimate love in our close relationships. Seek help from a qualified therapist in your own community. Contact the U.S. Association for Body Psychotherapy, the American Counseling Association, the American Psychological Association, a local mental health clinic or rape crisis center, a local domestic violence hotline, or another reputable national organization. Most organizations have web sites that offer a referral service and list detailed qualifications of affiliated therapists. Check the appendix of this book for more detailed information.

Don't Rescue Anyone

Many of us are not in an abusive relationship, but have fallen into a different kind of relationship trap. Are you a helper and savior who has fallen in love with a lost soul, someone who needs your help, who might not make it without you? The power to rescue another human being is a great aphrodisiac. Many of us have tried. Very few of us succeed. The prognosis is quite poor.

Needy people who claim they cannot function without our help usually would benefit from professional counseling. Even if in our profession we are a therapist, in our own personal love life, it is doubtful that we can cure or save another adult: a child perhaps, an adult, no.

By the time a man or woman is past their teens, their personality and character traits are well formed. Work habits, attitudes toward life, and approach toward achieving success are, for the most part, already determined. Will they succeed or won't they? Take a look at their track record. Observe their present condition. Talk to their friends and relatives. Pay attention to the words they say and the actions they take. Are they grounded in reality or creating unrealistic castles in the sky, someday in the future?

- *What's going on right now?*

- *Is this person planning for the future or expecting you to be the rock, the savior, and the escape valve?*

- *Does this person take personal responsibility or blame others for most problems?*

- *Does this person threaten self mutilation, suicide, or the intent to harm someone else, maybe you?*

Nobody can protect another adult around the clock. Do not keep these problems a secret. Inform someone close to you. Seek professional help and personal protection.

Not quite ready to give up on a difficult relationship? Still believe your partner has potential that has not yet been realized? Then give yourself a time period. Check back in six months. Check again in one year. Give yourself regular checkpoints. Take another look at yourself and your partner. It may be time to give up a losing battle. Love doesn't have to be difficult or painful. Love can be a healing, joyful and blissful partnership.

Getting Free

Sit quietly for awhile. Allow your mind to focus on your most significant relationship, past or present. If you like, you may repeat this exercise for different relationships. In your journal make two lists:

What I Have Given to the Relationship -- What I Have Received From the Relationship

When you have completed both lists, ask yourself the following questions:

- *How do I feel about myself in this relationship?*
- *How do I feel about my partner?*
- *What would have to happen for me to leave?*
- *What would have to happen for me to stay?*

Do you feel nurtured, pampered, special, honored, and respected? Then stay and languish in the pleasure. However, if you feel unhappy, frustrated, neglected, and insecure, it may be time to make some changes. Talk to someone who understands and can help. Attend codependency anonymous meetings. Sign up for a local lecture or course about relationships. See a professional psychotherapist, body oriented or somatic psychotherapist. Seek spiritual counseling from a local minister, rabbi or priest.

If you decide to stay, your relationship will not flourish if you are holding on to painful memories and explosive feelings. Body therapies can help your body to release the tensions that hold your emotions locked inside. Body psychotherapy can help you to uncover the deeper meanings in your own life.

Once you have truly acknowledged, experienced and released the painful emotions that have kept you stuck, you may finally be ready to forgive. Without forgiveness, we remain a victim of our feelings and maintain the sense of being less than whole. Forgiveness frees us to openly enjoy our life again.

We cannot **pretend** to forgive. If you are not ready to forgive, that's okay. Just admit the truth. Hold on to your anger, rage or sadness for as long as you need. When you are finally ready, six months or two years from now, you can return to this page and begin the forgiveness process. You will not regret it. In fact, after years of suffering, forgiveness can give you some closure and a sense of relief. After you have forgiven others, and most importantly, forgiven your self, you may finally be ready to create intimacy in your relationships.

Forgiveness

Can you honestly forgive your partner for the ways he or she has hurt or disappointed you?

List the ways your partner has hurt, disappointed, discounted or betrayed you?

Explain some possible reasons why this happened?

Describe what it will take for you to forgive your partner and for your partner to forgive him or her self.

Can you honestly forgive your self for the ways you have hurt or disappointed your partner?

List the ways you have hurt, disappoint, discounted or betrayed your partner?

Explain some possible reasons why this happened?

Describe what it will take for your partner to forgive you and for you to forgive your self.

Being Love

"Being love," a term coined by humanistic psychologist Abraham Maslow, is more important than merely showing and expressing love. Being love is being who you are. Being love is allowing the other to see you in all your shades of color, from beautiful tender pink to insecure, jealous green, to dark gray and even nasty black. Being love is also looking clearly at the other person, observing all their shades of emotion, feeling and expression.

What would it be like for you to experience **BEING LOVE** for one day, for one hour? Imagine freely saying what you feel, without needing to be right, good, bad, appropriate, or accepted?

Imagine your partner "being" love. Imagine seeing the full range of beauty and darkness inside your lover's mind and heart. Each of us holds within us thoughts and feelings, like barely perceptible but always threatening to destroy the moment, clouds. What would happen if, just for a few brief moments, we allowed our love, our being, to pour forth unhampered?

We often try to control another person by suppressing and inhibiting their natural way of being. Imagine allowing each other to "be love", free from the every day restrictions that keep us tied to half-truths and superficial images. Imagine allowing another the freedom to be fully him or her self, knowing they may say and do things that you would prefer not to hear or experience, knowing they may disappoint or even dishonor you. Imagine remaining internally confident, knowing who you are, no matter what the other person says or does. Imagine two people "being" love together in an intimate and sexual relationship. Imagine the physical, emotional and spiritual passion that could come forth. Sex would never be the same again. Would there be a need for any other?

Love Changes Everything

Love has a mind all its own. When hit by the "bug", the "victim" may appear to have suddenly gone insane. A woman with very high standards of etiquette may find herself paying for her man's dinners and even loaning him money. A man who has been a "stud" for years may find himself crooning over a woman who barely allows him to touch her. A sophisticated, successful married man may become involved with a stripper or call girl from a lower class and a different race.

How do you know if you're in love? One clue is that your logical, reasonable mind tells you to do one thing and your heart leads you on another path. Your mind tells you: "Danger. This relationship is not safe because ...."

But, whenever Mr. or Miss Danger calls, your former resolve melts and you go running to be with this person.

Is it worth pursuing love at all costs? For many people it is. Sometimes the path ahead is laden with pain and eventual loss. But taking the safer route, avoiding passion to select a logical, compatible partner, is not always the best choice. For some of us this may eventually lead to a sense of isolation, loneliness, even despair. At some point, we may betray our compatible partner to be with someone else who does inspire passion, and, of course, is not "safe".

If you are in a quandary, loving someone "not appropriate" but wanting someone "safe" to spend your life with, there **is** a solution. Speak to a professional about your confusion, someone who can provide counseling and give you a broader perspective. But talk therapy alone may not be the solution. The confusion, turmoil and indecision may result from memories, feelings and emotions that remain locked inside your body. **Touch therapy and body psychotherapy** may assist you to unlock the mystery of your own mind. Only when you have examined your own thought processes and connected with your own innermost feelings, can you begin to choose how you want to live your life and with whom.

The Basic Decision To Love

For most intimate relationships, there is one basic decision, **Do I want to be with this person or would I rather leave to find someone else?** Ask yourself the following questions. Answer as truthfully as you possibly can.

- Would I prefer to leave but I'm afraid of losing the security, money, or friendship of this person?
- Do I really want to stay but I'm afraid of admitting something -- I don't plan to finish graduate school, write that novel, make a million dollars, or have a baby?
- Am I afraid of revealing some deep, dark personal secret?
- Would I rather run away than take the chance of revealing myself and becoming close to someone who seems to care?

If your true desire is to leave, to run for your life, to find your own center, then find support to face the truth, plan your exit -- and -- **walk out the door!**

Do you want to stay? Do you really love this person? Do you feel passion and truly believe your life is better together than apart? Have you eliminated the red flags of abuse? Are you no longer seeking to rescue or be rescued by anyone? Then, begin to examine your motives, attitudes, expectations, and behaviors. Search for the underlying goodness of your partner. Find out how you can make your relationship work. Then don't worry what anybody else thinks or tells you is right or wrong. Do what you feel in your own heart is true for you. Do whatever it takes for both of your to feel the joy that is possible in a truly loving relationship.

What Is Intimacy?

Intimacy is being willing to tell your truth, moment to moment. Intimacy is also being willing to listen and to hear your intimate companions' truth, moment to moment, even when you are hearing things you would rather not know.

What does it take to create long-lasting, satisfying love? Long-time married couples would probably answer: "Hard work!" Newlyweds might say: "Passionate sex!" Others might add, "Money, financial security, a good home, vacations...."

How do we create long-lasting intimacy in our life within our current relationships? We begin by facing our self, admitting what we truly feel, want, desire and need. Depending upon our personality and lifestyle, we may choose talk therapy, body psychotherapy or self-help peer groups. It is never too late to learn to love and accept our self. It is never too late to love and accept others. Why not begin now? Learning to love takes time. How much longer do you want to wait for love?

Creating Intimacy

This exercise is designed for couples. If you are alone, sit facing yourself in the mirror, as if the person you see is your partner. Set aside a definite block of time, at least one hour per week, for one month.

Begin each session by placing your chairs face to face and closing your eyes. Breathe quietly, slowly, deeply and rhythmically. Open your eyes and gaze softly into your partner's eyes. Observe the subtle colors and movements. Smile openly. Gradually, allow your breathing to synchronize with your partner's breaths. Take turns asking each other the following questions. When it is your turn to respond, please answer as truthfully and kindly as you can.

- *Is there anything bothering you about me, our relationship, or your own personal life right now?*

- *Is there anything you would like me to change right now?*
- *What are you willing to change right now?*
- *What are you willing to accept or overlook right now?*
- *Is there anything you want to tell me or discuss with me right now?*

After the first person has responded to all the questions, the one who asked the questions should say, **"Thank you for sharing your truth with me."**

When both have responded to all the questions, smile, kiss and give each other a warm, tender, loving hug that lasts at least one minute.

Now, sit facing each other, continually gazing into each other's eyes.

For two minutes, take turns saying back and forth,

> **"Every moment we are together, I am discovering who you are."**

Then, one person keep repeating the following words, for two minutes, gently and

lovingly touching different body parts on your partner each time.

Insert your name or your partner's name where appropriate.

> **"Carol, you're a beautiful, sexy, powerful woman."**

> Or **"Sam, you're a handsome, sexy, powerful man."**

Each time, the listener responds by touching the partner gently and saying,

> **"Yes, I'm a beautiful, sexy, powerful woman"**

> Or **"Yes, I'm a handsome, sexy, powerful man."**

Copyright © 2009, Revised 2023   Love Me ... Please   DrEricaGoodstone.com

Finally, hold hands and gaze into each other's eyes.

>The first person says, **"In my heart, I am sharing my love with you."**
>
>The second person responds, **"In my heart, I am receiving your love."**
>
>The second person says, **"In my heart, I am sharing my love with you."**
>
>The first person responds, **"In my heart, I am receiving your love."**

Remember to breathe together as you gaze into each other's eyes.

Finish with a long kiss, an even longer hug, perhaps offering each other some massage and telling each other sweet nothings that you have both been longing to hear.

If these exercises don't stimulate or rekindle your love, perhaps it is time to say goodbye or maybe it is not too late for couples' therapist or marriage counselor to help. If not, if you are married and contemplating divorce, seeing a divorce mediator or divorce lawyer may be the next step. The choice is yours. How do you want to live your life:

- In anger, despair, confusion, and loneliness?
- In love, emotional closeness, pleasure and joy?

Lover's Bill Of Rights

Create your own Lover's Bill of Rights.

- *What do you believe are your rights as a lover?*

- *How do you want and expect your lover to behave?*

- *What do you believe are your lover's rights?*

- *How do you believe your lover wants and expects you to behave?*

It's The Little Things That Count

What do you focus on in selecting an intimate partner or lifetime mate? Many of us seek a partner who we believe will make our life easy, provide for us, pay our bills, and offer us gifts. For some of us, an exciting sexual relationship or an attractive partner we are proud to be seen with, is enough. For others a satisfying relationship is with a partner who builds and repairs things, a partner who cooks and cleans, someone who listens to our problems, plays with us when we're happy, or someone who hugs us when we are sad.

For most of us, some combination of all of the above, plus more, is what it takes to create and remain in a relationship. A popular song in the 1950's summed it up in the title: ***Little Things Mean a Lot.*** Each of us has those "little things" that may mean more to us than money, power, good looks, or sex. Choose a partner who naturally and easily does those little things. Sometimes a reluctant partner can learn, but more often, those little things become a sticking point as we spend extended periods of time with our partner.

Tell the truth to yourself. Do you have the patience to teach and persuade your partner to provide those little things for you? Or are you the no nonsense, quick fix type, who would rather switch than fight? Know yourself and decide. The choice is yours. Choose carefully. Your choice may remain with you for a lifetime!

It is an awesome responsibility to love another. Just as an infant depends on its caretaker for love, feeding and mirroring, when we fall in love as an adult, we become like an infant. In loving another, we allow our self to be emotionally affected. Our partner's words, actions, even thoughts, have the power to hurt us or uplift us, to make us angry, confused, sad or elated. Most of us do not even fathom the power we have to affect those we love. Isn't it time **you** learned to use your power wisely, with compassion and kindness for your self and for others?

FOOTNOTES

Chapter 1

1. Ornish, Dean, M.D. (1997). *Love and Survival: The Scientific Basis for the Healing Power of Intimacy.* New York: HarperCollins Publishers.
2. Schnarch, Ph.D. (1997). *Passionate Marriage: Sex, Love and Intimacy in Emotionally Committed Relationships.* New York: W.W. Norton & Company, Inc.
3. Mahler, Margaret S., M.D., Pine, Fred, Bergman, Anni. (1975). *The Psychological Birth of the Human Infant: Symbiosis and Individuation.* New York. Basic Books, Inc.

Chapter 3

1. Wayne, Dennis (1973). *Children of the Creche.* New York. Appleton-Century-Crofts.

CONGRATULATIONS!

You have finished the first chapter in Book 1. You have completed some powerful, life-transforming exercises. You have self-reflected and contemplated what you have and what you want in your life. And – you have revealed to yourself how you want to love and be loved. In this book you have gained an intimate knowledge of your own self – the ways you think, feel, behave, respond and influence the thoughts, behaviors and responses of others.

MORE TO COME!

Touch Me … Please

Touch Me … Please introduces the healing potential of simple touch, from a gentle touch on the shoulder by an acquaintance, to the warm fuzzy feeling you get when your favorite pet cuddles us to you, or the wondrously tingly sensations of your intimate lover's touch. This beautiful Ebook is sure to delight you with powerful real-life stories about the transformative power of touch, current research, abundant exercises for self-analysis and partner sharing as well as a full explanation of the wide variety of healing body therapies and healing somatic body psychotherapies.

Heal Me … Please

Healing happens in every moment, in every cell and organ of our body. Loving, touching, and being touched with love, we heal. When we heal, our bodies relax and our lives come into balance. In healing, we discover our own truth, face our inner spirit, and we begin to know our connection to a higher source. In ***Heal Me … Please*** we examine the healing process: what we believe about healing, how we have healed our self and others, and how we can create healing in our bodies, our intimate relationships, our sexuality, and our lives.

Sexual and Spiritual Reawakening

We are all sexual beings. Sexuality teaches. Sexuality heals. Sometimes our sexuality hurts. When we allow our hearts to feel love and our bodies to feel pleasure, we are sexual. Being sexual is being alive. Feeling our sexual aliveness reawakens us to who we are. By allowing full sexual expression into our life, we cannot help but discover our spiritual nature.

We are all spiritual beings. Connecting to our spiritual nature and spiritual potential brings us an accepting appreciation of life. The path of discovering our spiritual connection can be difficult, painful and may reveal to us our deepest, darkest, most unloving personal attributes.

Our life path is a spiritual path, the process of rediscovering our connection to all that is. No matter which direction we choose to take, all paths will eventually lead us home. Every spiritual teaching reminds us of that simple truth. If we resist knowing this truth and pursue a self-centered and purely material way of life, we may encounter more struggle, more difficulties, and more tests than necessary. But even if we do pursue a spiritual path, there are still obstacles and difficulties to be overcome. The difference is that knowing our spiritual essence provides emotional strength and calmness in the face of any stormy life issues, problems and concerns. ***Sexual and Spiritual Reawakening*** is a simple guide to help you live a more fulfilling, life affirming and joyful existence.

Have any of the words or exercises in this book touched a sensitive place in your thoughts, emotions or beliefs?

Are you ready to Lose

- **Your fears?**
- **Your doubts?**

Are you ready to Create

- **Love and healing?**

It's NOT Too Late!

NOW IS THE TIME TO CREATE HEALING AND LOVE IN <u>YOUR</u> LIFE!

LoveNow.life/HealingThroughLoveSession

ALSO BY DR. ERICA GOODSTONE

KINDLE BOOKS

Beautiful Bare Feet: Fetish or Fantasy
Be Who You Are: The Greatest Gift of All
The Delicate Dance of Love
Your Body Believes You
It's a Sensational World
Touching Matters - The Profound Effects of Body Therapy
Let All Your Senses Speak – As You Heal
Touching Stories
Ordinary People, Ordinary Yet Extraordinary Sex
Sexual Reawakening: 10 Simple Steps
Sexual and Spiritual Reawakening – At Last!
The Science Of Being Well - Wallace D. Wattles author,
 Annotated and Illustrated by Dr. Erica Goodstone
The Science Of Getting Rich - Wallace D. Wattles author,
 Annotated and Illustrated by Dr. Erica Goodstone

Books and EBooks are available at
Amazon.com, Smashwords.com and Lulu.com

DIGITAL PROGRAMS

Love Touch Heal Video Series
Healing Through Love Audio Series
Love Lessons For Your Soul
Love Touch Heal Relationship Program

VIRTUAL SUMMITS

Men and Love Series
Women and Love Summit
Sexual Reawakening Summit
Love Me Touch Me Heal Me Summit
Healing Recovery Retreat
Miraculous Healing Master Class Summit
Science And Poetry of Love Summit
The Science of Being Well Docuseries

Programs, courses and summits available at
https://DrEricaGoodstone.com

AMAZON REVIEWS

If you have enjoyed reading this book, please consider leaving an Amazon review. The author will be most grateful because this enables her to reach more people who want to create more love in their lives.

www.ingramcontent.com/pod-product-compliance
Lightning Source LLC
Chambersburg PA
CBHW080548170426
43195CB00016B/2720